RELIGION AND SOCIETY IN THE HIMALAYAS

Religion and Society in the Himalayas

Edited by
Tanka B. Subba
and
Karubaki Datta

GYAN PUBLISHING HOUSE
New Delhi - 110002

RELIGION AND SOCIETY IN THE HIMALAYAS

ISBN : 9788121203340

Published in 2015 in India by
Gyan Publishing House
5, Ansari Road, Daryaganj,
New Delhi - 110002
Phones : 23261060, 23282060 Fax : 23285914
e-mail : books@gyanbooks.com
website : gyanbooks.com

Laser Typesetting at : Vinayak Printers, Delhi
Printed at : Salasar Imaging System, Delhi

CONTENTS

Introduction

If any social scientist is asked to say about the most characteristic aspect of the Himalayas, then the answer would be 'religion'. Of course religion is an integral part of the non-Himalayan societies also, but there its role is rather disintegrative while in the Himalayan societies it is just as it should be—an integrating and cementing force.

The importance of religion in the Himalayan societies is immense though not much exploring has been done in this field. The earlier writers on the Himalayas have mostly been concerned with delving into the theosophical bases of religion, particularly Buddhism. The Tantic aspects of Buddhism as practised by the not-*Gelugpa* sects, have also attracted the attention of very many scholars recently. But the animistic religions of the Himalayas have received relatively lesser attention of scholars. Barring a few such works, confined to the southern Himalayas and descriptive accounts of the religious practices of the trives of Arunachal Pradesh, the rich field of the study of the religion has remained rather ignored. This is probably because the entire attention was directed towards Tibet—the destination of many a missionary and scholar right from the seventeenth century. But even in Tibet the religious studies are mostly confined to the elite Buddhist centres of learning, or the few urban and administrative centres. The Buddhism as it exists in more remote and more inaccessible parts of the eastern and north-eastern provinces has not been properly studied.

Such lapses are more pronounced in areas like Arunachal Pradesh, Sikkim and Darjeeling and in countries such as nepal and Bhutan. It was to fill this gap that the Centre for Himalayan Studies organised a national seminar on 'Religion and Society in the Himalayas' on March 13-15, 1986. Being an 'area study' centre, established especially for the study of Tibet and Bhutan, the focus of this seminar was on these countries though the hinterland areas of these could not be excluded in this regard. These two countries being still inaccessible for primary research, our Centre has been carrying on researches mainly on their hinterland - Arunachal Pradesh, Sikkim, eastern Nepal and Darjeeling—while preparing itself to enter into their heartlands as and when the situation would permit.

It is such a position of our Centre that compels it to collect and combine in one place the knowledge of the various people associated with the area/region of concern. The selection of the papers for this volume has been influenced mainly by this consideration of our Centre. Thus, of the twelve papers included here, seven of them centre around Buddhism, one on the interrelationship of Buddhism and Hinduism, one on Christianity, and the remaining three on the so-called 'animistic' religions. In terms of areas, there are two each on Tibet, Arunachal Pradesh and Sikkim and one on Nepal, Darjeeling and Bhutan, the remaing three being on the Himalayas in general.

The first paper by Professor S.K. Chaube, former Director of our Centre, deals with the relationship between religion and politics in Tibet. He points out how the *Mahayana* monasteries, which preponderate in the Himalayas, deprived the government of Tibet of a lot of tis secular functions and performed their roles which combined both the secular and the sacred. He illustrates his thesis with examples from non-Buddhist societies also but particularly with the *Gelugpa* sect. He also shows how the Tibetans had smoothly resolved the dichotomy between the sacred and the secular hierarchies.

The second paper by Dr. Dawa Norbu, a well known Tibetologist, deals with the comcept of 'Karma' and its application in Tibetan society. Though basically a political scientist, he ably brings out he sociological significance of 'Karma' not only as a mechanism of social control or a constraint on social behavour, but also as a motivation for better social living.

The third paper by Dr. Ringu Tulku, a 'reincarnated' monk, is probably the most authentic account of the Bon or the pre-Buddhistic rites of *Lhasang, Lalhu, Toh* and *Doo,* which the Buddhists have now accepted as their popular rites in the entire Himalayas. With the help of many an example, his paper shows how Buddhism has adapted itself to the Bon traits existing earlier but also how, in the rocess of doing so, it has adopted only those aspects which uphold the benevolent nature of the religion.

The fourth paper by Dr. Bina Roy Burman, a reputed Tibetologist, provides the total cultural landscape of the Indian Himalayas where the Buddhist societies live and thrive. She names the various sects to which these monasteries belong and then brings out the impact of modernasation and secular educatoin on them. She also shown how the dynamic leadership of the Dalai Lama has made the Tibetans more stable and forward looking today.

The fifth paper is by Profesor Trevor Ling, a sociologist and a Buddhist scholar of repute. He contends that the Sikkimese Buddhism of the nineteenth century had urban root and character developed in Tibet. The rise of Gorkha power on the west has been shown on the basis of the growth and distribution of monasteries in the nineteenth centrury Sikkim. He also deals with the problem of orientation faced by the Sikkimese monasteries due to the occupation of Tibet by China in 1959.

The sixth paper by Dr. Ranju Rani Dhamala is a case study of the socio-exonomic condition of the Pemayangtse Monastery of Sikkim. She has described in detail the personnel and the economy of the monastery and the changes forced on it by socio-political and exonomic realities. The paper presents the story of the survival of a tradition-bound monastery amidst the diverse challenges of the modern times.

Karubaki Datta's bibliographic notes on Tibet, Bhutan and Sikkim is the seventh paper which concludes the earlier papers on Buddhism in these regions. The various sources of literature have been classified and arranged thematically in an article form. She has shown the qualitative differences of the modern science researches on these regions from the earlier publications which were either travel accounts or philosophical discourses on the Buddhism of Tibet.

The eighth paper is by Professor Gopal Singh Nepali, an authority on the Newars. In this paper, he presents numerous examples which bear testimony to the close interaction between buddhism and Hinduism in Nepal. Set in the structural-functional framework, he contends that Buddhism in Nepal has thrived because it has made both structural and functional adaptations to the caste system against which it had revolted in India.

In th ninth paper, Father George Kottuppallil, a Christian missionary himself, has given an authentic account of the spread of the Roman Catholicism in Darjeeling in the nineteenth century. On the basis of some rare documents and books collected from Rome, he shows that the strategy of both the Protestants and Catholics was basically the same-the spread of education-but the latter had to experience resistance offered by the British administration.

The tenth paper is by a very senior scholar on Arunachal Pradesh, J.N. Choudhuary. As expected of his stature his canvas is indeed broadm nonetheless intricately designed. He not only describes the religious beliegs and practices of Arunachal Pradesh in a detailed manner but also makes an overview of them at a theoretical plane.

The eleventh paper is by Dr. Tamo Mibang, an upcoming adi scholar. He has described and explained some of the rites and rituals of the Minyongs, a sub-tribe of the Adis. He has also shwn how *Donyi Poloism* is not only a form of religion but also a symbol of identity for them.

The last paper is by Bimalendu Majumdar, an active social worker. He has first hand knowledge of many tribal groups in North Bengal. His present paper on the Doyas of Bhutan shows a lot of socio-religious similarities not only the Totos who live close to them, but also with many other tribes of north-east India.

These twelve selected papers not only deal with some of the least researched regions and countries but also with one of the least explored fields of interdisciplinary research. Most of the authors are specialists in their own fields and hence the authenticity is unqestioned.

The selection-cum-editing of the paper was originally planned to be done by the two senior professor, S.K. Chaube and G.S. Nepali. But for various reasons, they could not see through the volume many of us eagerly looked forward to. Finally, the responsibility, which was perhaps too big for our stature, devolved upon us in late 1989.

After accepting the responsibility, we have taken full liberty of editing the selected papers and even editorialising some of them. Our editing mainly related to making the spellings, transliterations etc. consistent and the expressions clearer. It is primarily towards the total homogeneity of the papers that some of them have undergone drastic changes for which the concerned authors may kindly forgive us. The reference system too had to be drastically modified in some cases in spite of which absolute consistency has not been possible. We also regret that we could not provide complete reference wherever lacking but we have done the best we could.

In the task of transliteration, we have been greatly benefited by the cooperation extended by our friend and colleague Sri Ugyen C. Lama. We are thankful to him. Finally we thank Sri Ranjit Kumar for typing out the densely edited manuscript and taking extra trouble at that.

Needless to mention that the editors bear no responsibility for the opinios expressed or facts presented by the authors. However, we bear full responsibility for editorial lapse that may have remained.

Tanka Bahadur Subba and Kurubaki Datta

CONTRIBUTORS

S.K Chaube	Professor of Political Science, Delhi University, Delhi.
Dawa Norbu	Associate Professor, School of International Studies, Jawaharlal Nehru University, New Delhi.
Ringu Tulku	Lecturer in Tibetan, Sikkim Government College, Tadong, Sikkim
Bina Roy Burman	Post-Doctoral Fellow, ICSSR, New Delhi.
Trevor Ling	Professor of Sociology,Singapore National University, Singapore.
Ranju R. Dhamala	Reader, Centre for Himalayan Studies, North Bengal University.
Karubaki Datta	Lecturer, Centre for Himalayan Studies, North Bengal University
Gopal Singh Nepali	Professor, Department of Sociology and Anthropology, Tribhuvan University, Kathamandu, Nepal
G. Kottuppallil	Librarian, Sacred Heart College, Shillong
J.N.Chowdhury	Retired Librarian, Arunachal Research Department Library, Shillong.
Tamo Mibang	Reader in History, Arunachal University, Pasighat, Arunachal Pradesh.
Bimalendu Majumdar	Freelance Researcher, Silpasamitipara, Jalpaiguri.

CHAPTER 1

Religion and Politics in Tibet

S.K.Chaube*

Temples and Monasteries

The great Sanskrit poet Kalidasa called the Himalayas 'devatatma' and a modern Indian geographer, S.C. Bose, writes that "in the Himalayas there are hundreds of temples and shrines sacred to the Hindus and other religions".[1]

Besides this popular image of the Himalayas as the abode of gods which must have led to the foundation of several temples and shrines in the Himalayan ranges, the fact that the Himalayas are the habitat of a diverse set of peoples with distinctive religions and cultures must go to explain the existence of several other places of religious importance.

It needs, however, to be noted that pilgrimage to the Himalayas from the Indian plains is almost exclusively confined to the Hindus. Except for the temple of Swayambhunath in Nepal the Buddhist shrines in the Himalayas attract very few pilgrims. The Buddhist pilgrimage sites are mostly confined to places in the plains of India (Bodh Gaya, Nalanda, Saranath, *etc.*).

This fact may point out a significant phenomenon in the Mahayana School of Buddhism. Whereas the places associated with the Buddha's

* Professor of Political Science, Delhi University, Delhi.

own life are objects of attraction, the monasteries themselves hardly serve as the pilgrim spot. Their functions are not only religious but also social, economic and administrative. Beyond its specific jurisdiction the monastery hardly has a function.

Within its jurisdiction the monastery primarily serves as the residence of the monks. In the second place, in the Buddhist Tibet, Sikkim and Bhutan, they are also linked with the administrative headquarters. In the third place, the location of the existing monasteries would suggest their linkage with trans-Himalayan trade. The Hindu pilgrimage centres of course provided for shelter of monks and hermits. They even served as exchange centres. But both these functions are technically 'non-organized'. And beyond the range of a temple's estate/property the temple has no administrative function.

On the basis of this preliminary information a hypothesis can be developed that the Mahayana monasteries take away a large part of the secular functions of the government. At the same time it cuts into the religious importance of the temple. The monks, thus, emerge as a special caste exercising authority over both the sacred and the secular affairs of the society.

The sacred and the secular

The point may be clarified in this way. In the ancient Hindu polity, the Brahmin caste had some specific socio-political function. This function, however, did not belong to the priests of any temple except for offering blessings of personal nature. The phenomenon is observed in the only surviving Hindu kingdom in the world—Nepal.

On the other hand, in Sikkim, the monastic lamas discharged specific political functions beginning from consecration of a king to even fighting in wars. In Bhutan every *Dzong* has a lamasery in it and the lamas are substantially represented in every part of the polity. In the *Gelugpa (dGe-Lugs-Pa)* Tibet the lamas were the rulers. The Tibetan case is the extreme example of convergence of religion and politics, comparable only to the Islamic political order under the Prophet Muhammed (The subsequent *Khilafat* pattern of course represents divine right monarchy rather than the identity of the religious and the temporal head of polity).

Even the Holy Roman Empire did not acknowledge the temporal supremacy of the Pope, though his backing was essential to a Christian king. The Prophet Muhammad led a transformation from a tribal social order to a statehood of the Arab people with the Holy Quran and the sword in his two hands. But the political authority of the *Gelugpa* chief in Tibet was not primarily based on his military strength. In fact, the Buddhist doctrines do not strictly permit a monk to be a ruler.

This of course raises the problem of explaining the so-called 'Buddhist' rulers like Asoka. A great deal of controversy centres on Emperor Asoka's connections with the Buddhist sect. The phrase *Sanghe upete* may, however, be explained if we take the view of early Buddhism as an intellectual movement rather than a creed. It is possible to assume that Asoka, at a certain stage of his life, chose to live in the *Sangha* (monastery) and then return to his throne and family. The interchangeability of the monastic and the mundane life in an individual's life history persists in the Theravada tradition and may be identified even in some Mahayana sects. Ngwang Namgyal's (founder of Bhutan) own life reveals their interchangeability.

Gelugpa authority in Tibet

The *Gelugpa* sect, however, was a puritan reformist movement built around the concept of a life-long monkhood and celibacy. Its ascendancy to political power in Tibet is associated with the Mongol dominance.

There were, however, two stages of this identification of the sacred and the secular in Tibet. From the seventh century to the middle of the thirteenth century Tibet was under the authority of lay rulers. In 1251 Prince Godan, a grandson of Ghengis Khan, made the grand lama of the *Sakya (Sha-skyabs)* Sect, Kunga Gyaltsen *(Sakya Pandita)* his viceregent *(Tisri)* in Tibet. In 1253, Lodo Gyaltsen *(Phagpa)*, nephew of *Sakya Pandita,* was bestowed religious sovereignty over Tibet. The *Sakya* authority however, lapsed after the death of Kunga Gyaltsen but the Mongols, with reduced influence retained interest in Tibet which now passed under the control of lay rulers.

The political power of the *Gelugpa* sect in Tibet was the product of an alliance between the monks and the Mongol rulers. The third lama of the sect (flowing from Tsongkhapa) was awarded the title of Dalai Lama

(*Talao* = sea/ocean) by Altan Khan, the Khoshot/Tumet Mongol chief of Amdo in the Kokonor region. The *quid pro quo* seems to have been the acknowledgement of the son of a Chokur tribal chief of Mongolia and a great grandson of Altan Khan as the fourth Dalai Lama. The fifth Dalai Lama (Ngwang Lobsang Gyatso) was patronized by the Khoshot Mongol chief, Ghusri Khan, who conferred on him the title of the Supreme Religious Head of Tibet. The Mongol chief assumed the title of *Po Gyalpo* (virtuous king of Tibet), retained the power over defence and created the office of *Desi* (Regent) as the head of secular administration of Tibet. The title of the *Po Gyalpo* was passed down to Lhasang Khan, the last Mongol king of Tibet who was killed by the Jungar Mongols in 1717.

China and Tibet

The political relation between China and Tibet is largely shrouded by the mystique of the Chinese conception of sovereignty. The fact that Srongsen Gampo once sent an emissary to China and married a Chinese princess is considered in Chinese chronicles as evidence of Tibet's ancient subordination to China. The fact that the Mongols conquered Tibet as well as China and, subsequently, several Mongol groups came under Chinese control is cited with the same aim. On the other hand, the fall of the Ming dynasty in China certainly reduced Chinese authority in Tibet until the fifth Dalai Lama's advent. The fifth Dalai Lama visited China, but declined to assist the Manchu emperor in a war, and yet acknowledged the 'relationship of patronage' between the Manchu emperor and Tibet. The establishment of the Dalai Lama as the secular head of the country went through a triangular tussle of power. The Manchu king claimed sovereignty over the Khosot Mongol chief Ghusri Khan stationed in Tibet. The *Gelugpa* hierarchy tried to bypass the Mongol chief's authority. More than a decade after the Fifth Dalai Lama's death in 1695, Sangye, claiming to be delegate of the fifth Dalai Lama, sent an emissary to China seeking a Chinese official rank for the Dalai Lama. The rank of a 'prince' was conferred on him.

The Fifth Dalai Lama has proclaimed the principle of 'incarnation' of the Dalai Lama seeking to indegenize that institution. The leaking out of the information about the fifth Dalai Lama's death roused suspicion in the Manchu king's court. The Mongol chief at Lhasa utilized this opportunity to dismiss the sixth Dalai Lama chosen by Sangye and the Qing court ordered the latter's arrest who died on route to Beijing.

There was a temporary hegemony of the Mongol chief in Tibet. The Qing emperor sent a vice-minister (*Shilang*) in 1709 to rule Tibet jointly with the Mongol chief. Nor was the Mongol chief's nominee to the throne of Dalai Lama acceptable to the Tibetans. The *Gelugpa* hierarchs chose another monk as the sixth Dalai Lama (making altogether three Dalai Lamas in Tibetan history) whom the Qing court acknowledged.

The Khoshot Mongols' control over Tibet ended in 1717 with the invasion of the Jungar Mongols who killed Lhabzang Khan. The Chinese military interventions against the Jungar Mongol invasions ended the latter's power and gave Tibet a really autonomous rule. The next military interventions of the Chinese took place in 1728 in the context of an internecine war in the Tibetan ruling elite and, in 1792, against Gorkha invasion. The Chinese had placed an *Amban* (viceroy) at Lhasa in 1751 but left administrative authority in the hands of the *Gelugpa* hierarchs. The post of the *Amban* remained operative till the fall of the Qing dynasty when Tibet was embroiled in a fresh imperialistic assault. The Dalai Lama, who had so far enjoyed the patronage of the Qing emperor, now inclined on British support.

Religion and Politics

The purpose of this brief discussion is to seek to discover the forces that worked behind the very special political institution of the world that was wholly based on religious authority. The theoretical significance of the finding is that beyond the range of a 'tribal polity' it is not possible for a sacred hierarchy to enjoy independent political power. Its operative implication may be that the political distinctiveness of the Tibetan people may not be justified by religious authority of the Dalai Lama who derived his secular authority either from the Mongols or from the Chinese or from the British.

The dichotomy is compounded by the existence of a second focus of authority in Tibet—the Panchen Lama. On the day of the foundation of the People's Republic of China (PRC) the Panchen Lama is reported to have sent a wire to Mao Zedong expressing his support for the central authorities and his eagerness for the achievement of the motherland's unification and Tibet's liberation at an early date.[2] In the early days of the regime the government of the PRC tried to make direct appeals to the people of Tibet. In October 1950 the People's Liberation Army wiped out a 5000 strong Tibetan army. In the next spring the Regent over the fourteenth Dalai Lama stepped down and a Tibetan delegation reached Beijing to negotiate Tibet's union. On May 23, 1951 the agreement of the Central People's Government and the Local Government of Tibet on Measures for the Peaceful Liberation of Tibet was signed.

The agreement was delightfully ambiguous for China. By paragraph 4 of the Agreement the Central authorities undertook not to alter the political system of Tibet. But then, by paragraph 2 of the same agreement, the Tibetan authorities were recognized as the Local Government. By paragraphs 4 and 5 the Central authorities undertook to respect the established status of the Dalai Lama as well as the Panchen Lama. But, by 'the established status' paragraph 6 meant the status, functions and powers of the thirteenth Dalai Lama and the ninth Panchen Lama 'when they were in friendly and amicable relations with each other'.[3] This meant that the Dalai Lama alone was not supreme.

Paragraph 7 of the Agreement provided that 'the religious beliefs, customs and habits of the Tibetan people shall be respected and lama monasteries shall be protected. The Central authorities will not effect a change in the income of the monasteries'.[4] For the Tibetan religious hierarchy, therefore, there was an assurance of stability.

The Chinese revolution and Tibet

China had her first republican constitution adopted on September 20, 1954. Before that, on April 29, 1954 the Agreement of Trade and Intercourse between the Tibet Region of China and India was signed, settling the question of Chinese sovereignty on Tibet as far as India is concerned. This, apparently, caused some concern among the Tibetan hierarchs as evident in the visit of the Dalai Lama and the Panchen Lama.

In April 1956 the Preparatory Committee for the Tibet Autonomous Region was set up. In February 1957 Mao Zedong declared that 'it has now been decided not to proceed with democratic reforms in Tibet during the period of the Second Five Year Plan' (1958-62).[5] At the second session of the Eighth Congress of the Communist Party of China, however, the Great Leap Forward was undertaken. All the earlier cautions were thrown to the wind in China. The Tibetan hierarchy was nervous at the radical moves of the Central authorities. The result was the civil war in China and the Dalai Lama's escape. The 1959 events led to the abolition of the feudal and the monastic estates. Estates of the rebel monasteries were confiscated outright. These included the three great monasteries in Lhasa. On the other hand, the Tashi Lhungpo monastery, the seat of the Panchen Lama was paid some 9 million Yuan as compensation—the biggest compensation to any non-rebel estate-holder.[6] All political powers of the monasteries were abolished.

The revolution took a heavy toll of lamaism even in ecclesiastical terms. The Drepung monastery in Lhasa, for instance, which had an authorized strength of 9,777 lamas (occasionally exceeding 10,000 in practice), had its strength reduced to 715 in 1965, before the cultural revolution. The new economic order would simply not bear the monastic establishments.

The greatest ravage was done by the cultural revolution of 1966-76. All monasteries in Tibet except the Drepung monastery and the Potala palace were laid waste to varying degrees. Quite a few were reduced to ruins, among them the Gaden monastery, Lhasa's third largest. The strength of the Drepung lamasery fell to 306 in 1976, the last year of the cultural revolution.[7]

The damages of the cultural revolution are being restored but Tibet's economy is not, in the foreseeable future, likely to support the old gigantic monastic structure of rentiers. In 1983 an inmate of Lhasa's Jokhang monastery, the second biggest, reported:

> Virtually all the lamas here left during the 'cultural revolution'. In the past few years I have entered our monastery, plus 10 more who came just recently, making a total of just 21 lamas at present.[8]

By all accounts, the Chinese have ravaged the economic foundation of monasteries. They have been trying to build up the Panchen Lama as the alternative leader. Yet the Dalai Lama's moral authority seems to persist. Hence all the appeals to the Dalai Lama to return to Tibet.

Notes and References

1. S.C. Bose, (1979). *Geography of Himalaya* (New Delhi : National Book Trust, reprint), p.v.
2. Wang Furen and Suo Wenging, (1984). *Highlights of Tibetan History* (Beijing : New World Press), p.172.
3. *Ibid.*, p.186.
4. *Ibid.*, p.187.
5. Mao Zedong, (1957). *On the Correct Handling of Contradictions* (Peking; Foreign language press.)
6. Israel Epstein, (1983). *Tibet Transformed* (Beijing : New World Press), p.417.
7. *Ibid.*, p.424.
8. 'Tibet, Today & Yesterday', *China Today*, 7, (1983) p.35

CHAPTER 2

Karmic Ethos in Lamaist Society

Dawa Norbu*

The role of religion in maintaining social order, no matter how reactionary, cannot be underestimated. For without the regulation of life and social control exercised by religious ethics, we have to imagine a hypothetical situation in which the state has to put police at every doorstep. This social fact becomes increasingly evident in industrial societies where with the decline of religious influence, crime rate tends to increase at an alarming rate.

In this paper I discuss how the regulation of life and social control were exercised in Tibet by the Buddhist or Indic doctrine of Karma and reinforced by the notion of *Ngo-tsa*, a potent social norm peculiar to the Tibetans.[1] I argue that implicit in this religious doctrine is an irresistible social appeal to self-interest and self-responsibility as the basic motive of social action. Appeal to self-interest as an incentive to the observance of religious ethics may be implicit in most religious doctrines. But what characterizes the Tibetan Buddhist conception of Karma is their application of the doctrine not only to life after death but to social life here and now, which had made it really consequential. This human dimension of karma largely accounted for the success with which social order was

* Associate Professor, School of International Studies, Jawaharlal Nehru University, New Delhi.

maintained as well as how it influenced the structure of social action in lamaist society.

A traditional society like Tibet had none of the complex organizations, legal structures and above all state's coercive power with which a modern society functions. Tibet, for example, had no police force until the 1920s when the 13th Dalai Lama in his endeavour to modernize the country introduced a small force in Lhasa, but it "proved so unpopular that only a remnant is now left".[2] Nor did Tibet have much of a standing army. As Ekai Kawaguchi observed, "The standing army of Tibet is said to consist of five thousand men, but from my observation I think this number is somewhat exaggerated. In any case, it is hardly sufficient to protect a country containing six millions of inhabitants against foreign invasion and civil commotion. However, in Tibet social order is not kept by soldiers nor by the despotic power of the ruler. Religion is the force that keeps the country in good order".[3]

Indeed Tibetan history is characterized by a conspicuous lack, if not absence, of peasant revolts or general social unrest.[4] This seems an anomaly because of three factors that should have been conducive in generating social unrest : (a) economic exploitation, (b) the poor power basis of the lamaist regime, and (c) the primitive communication systems which made organized social control problematic. What made Tibetan society function orderly and smoothly was not so much structure or organization that has become the bane of social sciences today; it is the internalization and valorization of certain Buddhist ideas and values that were sacred yet practical to the Tibetan. It is true that no society function without social order which implies hierarchy and social stratification in general. However, given the extremely limited political means of enforcing these "rules of the game", the question arises : How did Tibetan society work in the way it did? What all this implies is a certain degree of internalization of values so that members of society act in a predictable manner through their shared meanings derived from religion.

Definition of 'Karma'

Since *Mahayana* Buddhism, to which the Tibetans adhere is a most complex religion, can we pinpoint a certain Buddhist doctrine that formed the core of this functioning value system in Tibet? At first sight Robert Redfield's "great tradition" and "little tradition"[5] seems applicable because as in most societies, you could find in Tibet scholarly and popular forms of Buddhism. Sociologically this kind of distinction shows only different degrees of cultural sophistication and not different kinds of specific religious ideas or values. What I mean by an operative value system is a certain set of sacred social norms derived from a world religion that transcend class division or levels of cultural sophistication in a given society.

Professor Giuseppe Tucci, on his numerous visits to the Tibetan world, got the impression that the Buddhist philosophical concept of *Sunyata* (Tib. *Stonpa nid*) was what influenced the Tibetan most. He wrote, "I think the most distinctive characteristic the Tibetan derived from his Buddhist faith was a sense of the fundamental vanity of things. From caravaneer to abbot, from peasant to lord, all shared the conviction that the world is *Tongpanyi* emptiness stripping all substantiality from what we think of as being, which is nothing but appearance".[6]

Tongpanyi (*sTon-Pa-Byiol*) or *Sunyata* is indeed one of the central doctrines of *Mahayana* Buddhism, but that was what lamas studied in monasteries and not necessarily what influenced the average Tibetan most. If that were the case, most Tibetans should have quit *Samsara,* which may be defined, from our perspective, as society. Leaving aside the caravaneer, the peasant and the lord, the Tibetan abbot's deep attachment to "good things of life" could not be explained. No traveller to Buddhist Tibet would quarrel with the fact that high lamas lived in such magnificence and opulence that resemble Chaucer's description of medieval bishops in England.[7] *Tongpanyi* cannot explain this social phenomena. For *Madhyamaka* philosophy postulates in essence that nothing, animate or inanimate, exists in the phenomenal world either by itself or in itself; there is no inherent existence as such. Translated into the domain of social mores it would amount to spurning of all that is alluring as there is nothing worthwhile striving for, and why should we be ensnared in worldly things.

However, I would concede that the concept of emptiness might have had a moderating effect on the sense of attachment to property, and perhaps provide an extreme philosophical basis for compassion which was the social lubricator of inter-personal relations in Tibet. But this concept was not a "socially determining" force. Nor could it give a satisfactory interpretation of social action. For the sociological implications and indeed social consequences of any action performed according to *Sunyata* would be either an anarchic nihilism or total world rejection, neither of which prevailed in Tibet. It is precisely for this reason that *Sunyata* was not publicly preached or propagated in Tibet; it was the exclusive domain of *Geshe,* most learned lamas.

If I were to single out a Buddhist principle that governed Tibetan social action, I would mention what we call in Tibetan *Ledre* (*Las 'Bras*), meaning literally and accurately "action and its result"—karma. This religious principle, as I shall try to show, was reinforced by a social norm called *Ngo-tsa* that might be roughly rendered as "losing face". Any social action contrary to *Ledre* would be interpreted as a violation of *Ngo-tsa* as well. Before I demonstrate the dynamics of these two mutually re-inforcing principles, let me quote a *lay* Tibetan who could not be accused of being either a "Westernized" Tibetan like this author or a lama who might not be representative of the average lay person. In his history of Tibet, Shakabpa makes the following comment ; "Tibetans lean strongly on their Buddhist faith and believe in the doctrine of karma; which teaches that the rewards and punishments of this life are the result of one's actions in the previous life. This is one of the reasons why Tibetans are very sympathetic, honest, cheerful, and satisfied with their lot".[8]

Even a Tibetan Muslim bases his whole treatise, *Kache Phalu' Rnamthar,* on the notion of karma. Though critical of certain Buddhist precepts, the author demonstrates his full agreement with the notion of karma and writes, "keep the doctrine of karma in mind, relate to others accordingly. Keep the principle of good and bad in mind, and perform your deeds accordingly".[9]

In his memoirs, the XIV Dalai Lama gives a similar definition of Karma. I shall again quote him. The intention is not so much to corroborate my proposition; it is to present the concept as the believers see it. "We believe with good reasons that all beings of various forms (both animal and human) are reborn after death. In each life, the proportion of peace and happiness which they experience is determined by their positive or negative deeds in the life before, although they may modify the proportion by their efforts in their present life. This is known as the law of Karma. Beings may move up or down in these realms, for example from animal to human life or back. Finally, by pure virtue and enlightenment, they may achieve *Nirvana*, when they cease to be reborn. Within *Nirvana*, there are various stages of enlightenment, the highest of all being Buddhahood".[10]

Finally, the findings of a Tibetan anthropologist confirm the continued vitality of the belief in Karma among Tibetan refugees. He lists incidences in which people attribute the various outcomes of their action or event to Karma; (a) one's misfortunes as "karmic backlash"; (b) one's fortune as positive karmic result.[11]

The karmic paradigm as the Dalai Lama's definition implies is meant to apply to "all sentient beings". We shall, however, discuss it from a purely sociological perspective as a popular projection of human desires, and for this reason I exclude rebirth below humans as an unlikely human aspiration. The paradigm defines the human condition as *Samsara* (society) which in realistic terms prepares us for problems of life and says in effect that society is not a rose garden; it interprets social action according to the logic of karma, *i.e.* different degrees of 'good' and 'bad'; finally it points to a transcendental goal (*Nirvana*) that ranges from a Buddhahood to a human rebirth, which in turn again ranges from a prince to a peasant. It is this complex gradation of options that makes karma more credible doctrine than others that simply offer either Heaven or Hell choice. Moreover, the dynamics of the whole paradigm and the law determining the continuous process of life is invested in the law of karma itself and this law makes every person responsible for his social action.

Every action will bear *in due course* its corresponding result, but the critical question of *when* exactly the action will ripen itself into its corresponding result is never spelled out. It may ripen sometimes in this life or in the next life time, but ripen it must when conditions are ripe. Herein lies the genius of the doctrine, to specify this timing would be not only to deprive its generality, but to dig its own grave. This critical question is made contingent upon the practice of Buddhism. "A seed of karma never dies. Unless it is eliminated by the practice of *Dharma* such a seed is dormant until the right conditions bring about its germination".[12]

What is the degree of autonomy that an individual acting under the forces of past karma can enjoy in his present actions that will determine his future rebirth? This question, somewhat similar to the Christian debate about freewill and destiny, is also not clearly answered. In more general terms lamas explain that once you happen to be born in a society where *Dharma* flourishes, then you have the fortune and freedom to learn "skilful means" to achieve positive karma. In order for a layman to acquire the "skilful means", in society the role of the lama (*guru*) was greatly stressed in Tibet for it was argued that without a lama there can be no Buddha.[13] When a society is turned up to the spirit of *Dharma*, a lay person's skilful means of ensuring good karma for his next life lay in conforming to the social order. That is not to kill, steal, or commit adultery, *etc*.

In the very vagueness or creative ambiguity of the doctrine lies in the seeds for the "general order of existence". There ample room is left for the leading role of lamas and the individual's responsibility to know the law. In maintaining that the result of an action may come about some time in this life or next, karma made itself relevant and consequential to social life here and now as well as to the hereafter. In maintaining that an individual acts partly under the forces of his past karma and partly independently under the light of *Dharma* the law of karma made its adherents independent as well as dependent. At first therefore the Buddhist appears as a "self-determining individualist' because he does not depend on divine grace for his liberation; everything depend on his action. In actual fact he is a "socially-determined being" because the quality of his action and therefore his whole future is determined by the degree to which he conforms to the *Dharma* which is a universal order, a series of self-explanatory "should dos" and "should not dos". Instead of making a long list of don't dos', the law makes its adherents responsible for what they do by giving them a high stake in their future as well as present life. Karmic ethics does not scare people to do the desired deeds; it induces them to do what is ethnically and socially acceptable by appealing to their self-interest.

The logic of karma provides ample space and freedom to its adherents to move around a meaningful moral pivot. It is not a simple matter of going to either heaven or hell. Karma is a most inclusive paradigm that claims to govern the life of every sentient being, from the smallest insect to the Buddha. If we view this law from a sociological perspective, as indicated earlier, the paradigm has two broad realms, *Nirvana* and *Samsara*, divine and human, if you will. Now within each of these two categories are numerous subcategories to choose from. If a world weary person wants "liberation" he could aim at a wide range of divine goals—Buddha, Buddhisatva, Deva, *etc*. On the other hand, if a person "who loves the green earth", wants a human rebirth, he could aim at the countless goals in life too familiar to us. There is then a vague precision about what you will gain or lose for what you have done. Tibetan texts are quite clear on specific prerequisites for specific human rebirth, as we shall now see.

Given such a wide range of options, a man is likely to emphasize where his nature inclines. Preference for human rebirth may be a foolish choice from the Buddha's point of view but it was certainly not a rejection or negation of the Buddha-seed said to be inherent in every sentient being. This very choice would be interpreted as an act of karma. In fact, for the simple Tibetan folks to aim at the Buddhahood seemed not only unrealistic but sacreligious. The notion of godhead was very much prevalent among the peasants and nomads, despite a millennium of god-denying Buddhism. In other words, to return to earth, if you do not mind "suffering", was no sin in the theological sense, you have merely delayed your journey towards Buddhahood.

Karma ana Self-interest

I shall go so far as to argue that the Buddhist missionaries in their endeavour to win *flocks*, especially those in power, emphasized the human dimension of the karmic ethos. This constitutes the substance of a whole corpus of literature called *Legshed* (*Leqs bShad*) that remains practically unexplored. *Leg-shed* literally means "well said", and it is the Buddhist canon for those in *Samsara*. This genre of literature, neither colloquial nor philosophical, is written in clear literary Tibetan and is literally the Buddhist handbook for laymen. Such literature gives the common man practical moral precepts and tips regarding the vital question of how to cope with life and how to get along with one's fellowmen. It also gives advice to princes about how to govern their kingdoms in accordance with the basic Buddhist tenets. Predominant themes of *Leg-shed* literature operate within the perimeters of karma; the recognition and upholding of the law of karma is insisted upon for the benefit of all beings.[14]

Secondly, Buddhist conversion strategy also seems to be based on popular appeals to karma. It is well known how Buddhism spread to various parts of Asia with the support of merchants; religion indeed travelled by trade routes. A less known case seems to be the worldly way in which the Buddhist missionaries sought to convert kings and princes. The traditional Buddhist strategy of proselytizing seems to have been aimed at converting the royal family, and if that was successful, the king would do the rest. The same strategy was employed against the early Tibetan kings in the seventh-eighth centuries A.D. A few centuries later the Tibetan high lamas would employ the same strategy to convert the Mongol in the thirteenth and seventeenth centuries.[15]

As opposed to the world-rejecting tone of the theoretical Buddhist canons, the type of literature addressed to rulers called *Shrulekha* (Furstenspiegel) is similar to *Leg-shed* intention but of course written in highly honorific language. It says to the effect : O, King ! you are mighty and fortunate. Thanks to your past karma. But if you use your present fortune in the "right way"(*i.e.* the Buddhist way) you could become an even greater king here on earth as well as ensure for yourself a bright future in life after death. It was not necessary for the king, it should be noted, to give up his kingdom. This is how an eminent Tibetan lama, Chogyal Phagpa (1235-1280), wrote to the Yuan Emperor Shih-tsu in 1271:

> O Lord of human beings!
>
> The time you should make (religious) effort is now.
> Make firm the good fortune you already have;
> ensure long life and the success of your lineage
> and practice methods to gain liberation.
>
> It is right to make efforts without distraction.
> At a time when Dharma has not yet set like a sun
> and when Dharmaraja like yourself sits on the throne,
> how can your kind remain indifferent to the plight of those who wear saffron robes?[16]

This is not an isolated case; Tibetan lamas have a long tradition that goes back to Indian Buddhist precedents. To mention a few well known Indian works of such a nature : Nagarjuna's *Rajaparikatha Ratnamala* and *Shrulekha* (both addressed to a Satavahana king); Chandragomin's

Shishyalekha and Matreeta's letter to king Kanishka. *Rajaparikhatha Ratnamala's* popularity in Tibet may be gauged by the fact that when the present Dalai Lama was asked to select a few Tibetan texts for "The Wisdom of Tibet Series" by a British publisher, he chose it.

From the point of view of our inquiry one of the most striking features of this text is the vivid and earthy, if not vulgarized manner in which the author tries to persuade the king to believe in the law of karma. This makes a good use of psychology by strongly appealing to human desires rather than to divine aspirations.

> Through the proper honouring of reliquaries,
> Honourable beings, superiors and the elderly
> You will become a Universal Monarch...
>
> Through never doing harm and freeing the condemned
> Beautiful will be your body, straight and large,
> Very tall with long fingers
> And broad backs of the heels.[17]

The book categorically enumerates in a hundred and one imaginable ways how specific qualities or conditions of life are caused by specific acts done in the past, thus implicitly urging : if you want to be born a handsome men, don't be jealous in this life, *etc*.

> A short life comes through killing,
> Much suffering through harming,
> Through stealing poor resources,
> Through adultery enemies.
>
> From lying arises slander,
> A parting of friends from divisiveness,
> From harshness hearing the unpleasant,
> From senselessness one's speech is not respected.
>
> Covetousness destroys one's wishes,
> Harmful intent yields fright,
> Wrong views lead to bad views,
> And drink to confusion of the mind.

> Through not giving comes poverty,
> Throgh wrong livelihood, deception,
> Through arrogance a bad lineage,
> Through jealousy little beauty.
>
> A bad colour comes through anger,
> Stupidity from not questioning
> The wise. The main of all this fruit
> is a bad migration for humans.[18]

The fourteenth Dalai Lama, when he wrote a poetic eulogy to Mao Zedong in 1954, was very much in this Buddhist missionary or diplomatic tradition. The Lama described the communist leader as "the Chakravarti born out of boundless fine merits". The hymn which now hangs in the central shrine of the Buddhist Temple of Broad Charity in Beijing reads in part:

> O! Chairman Mao! Your brilliance and deeds are like those of Brahma and Mahasamma, creators of the world.
>
> Only from an infinite number of good deeds can such a leader be born, who is like the sun shining over the world.[19]

It is interesting to note that even in this poem addressed to a declared atheist, Mao's present status as a great leader was attributed to his past "infinite number of good deeds" done in his previous lifetimes.

This pragmatic approach to play up the human dimension of the karmic ethos so as to appeal to human desires continues now in a new guise in the West. Tibetan lamas who found their way to the West from their exile in India preach to their followers in a similar tone. I quote from a booklet that seems to have become one of the bibles for those interested in Tibetan Buddhism. In his *The Preliminary Practices of Tibetan Buddhism,* Geshe Rapten preaches the following on the operation of the law karma:

> The main causes for rebirth as a human are restraint from killing and the pure observances of morality. If you refrain from stealing and harming people, and practice giving (dana), your life will be endowed with all the necessary material facilities. If you have

> dignity and independence, this is mainly the result of abandoning pride and practicing humility and respect, while the practice of patience is the main cause for a sound body.[20]

One could still go on quoting but it is probably enough to indicate firstly that there is a human dimension to the karmic ethos and secondly, that in their preachings to the lay followers, Buddhist missionaries do emphasize that human aspect in an obvious attempt to get the message across. "Change will come", says Geshe Rapten, "gradually after years of practice because our self-cherishing attitude is so deeply rooted that it seems part and parcel of our human nature".[21] As an elementary knowledge of psychology would show (and lamas are good natural psychologists), one of the best ways to convince people, especially the uninitiated, is to relate the doctrine to the level of human experience. It should not be misconstrued that what I have quoted was all that the lamas preached nor was that the only thing the Tibetans absorbed. This is indeed one of the dangers involved and for this reason I have mixed feelings about the value of quotations for elucidation. My only intention, however, is to focus on an aspect of karma that to my knowledge and experience, had deeper resonance in human psychology at any rate, in Tibet. A lama may indeed preach the entire "Four Noble Truths" and the law of karma with all its imaginable possibilities of rebirth, but it does not mean that his congregation might have absorbed all equally well. They may take a particular note when it rings a bell, and the bell rings the loudest usually when it appeals to human interest as such.

It would be unfair to conclude from our brief discussion that lamas manipulate human desires rather than uplift earthlings towards the otherwordly direction. Lamas felt perfectly justified in what they did. When I recently expressed my amazement at the frank appeal to human desires that Nagarjuna in his *Rajaparikhatha* makes, the lama replied without hesitation : "That is a skilful means". One of the Buddha's attributes is indeed *Thabkhey* - or *Thaba-mkhas*, meaning one who is skilled in finding suitable ways and means. In other words, the end justifies the means provided the means so used do not violate the basic tenets of the end. No ignoble means should be used to obtain a noble end. Lamas generally point out that the Buddha taught several levels and different ways of gaining enlightenment so that each individual or group of individuals, depending on his/their intelligence and determination could find a method that suits their respective levels. However, soon working consensus emerged in Tibet that suggested that those aspects of religion which have deeper resonance in human interest tended to gain greater mass appeal. Hence, the emphasis on the human dimension of the karmic ethos.

Implicit, then, in the general Buddhist doctrine and in particular in the law of karma is a realistic recognition of man's innate self-interest in this way : If you want to become a Buddha, Buddhisatva or to be reborn as a prince, a rich man *etc.* you have to do certain things. The law of karma tells you exactly what to do. Thus, while denying the existence of God controlling man's fate, karma in effect plays up man's ego, which is ironic because Buddhism is dedicated to the destruction of man's ego. Such psychological implications would have led to serious amoral and asocial consequences had it not been for an imperative condition that Buddhism laid for the realization of its promises : compassion. As a contemporary work states :

> Compassion enables one to realise one's objectives;
> Compassion enables others to realise their objectives;
> Compassion saves one from fear;
> And compassion makes friends.[22]

The law of karma makes the realization of man's self-interest contingent upon the practice of "good deeds". In what follows we shall discuss the place of compassion in the karmic paradigm and see how this value was internalized in Tibet.

Karma and Compassion

With the triumph of economic ideology in most industrial societies, traditional morality derived from religion had practically ceased to be a moral force governing life in society. This makes any academic discussion of terms like compassion, benevolence a suspect. Yet without understanding the objective role of compassion in social relations in a traditional society like Tibet, we would miss the underlying dynamics of society; how it works and why. In a hierarchical society where inequality is consecrated, the normative function of compassion or benevolence is as crucial as that of equality and liberty in an individualistic society. Equality and liberty are considered to be inalienable rights of an individual to be demanded legally, whereas compassion is seen as a religious duty to be socially expected.

Compassion in the karmic sense should not be understood in an altruistic sense; it is an instrumentalist act—one might say almost a selfish act - for the sake of sheer clarity. For one's whole future depends on one's present actions : if you want a good rebirth, you better do more good deeds. Compassion, largely understood as merit-saving activity, is a *means* to achieve good karma. As the Dalai Lama puts it "all true charity has a double benefit to the receiver in his present life, and to the giver in his present life or in his life to come."[23] This mode of reasoning, inculcated by the karmic paradigm, was internalized in Tibetans. Hence, the generosity that most Western travellers to Tibet found so overwhelming.[24] Hence, the poverty of the land too. Karmic ethos in the traditional setting was the inversion of the Protestant ethic.

> In the history of Tibet there is ample evidence for the vastness of the gifts and endowments devoted to the establishment or maintenance of temples and monasteries, and givers range from kings and tribal chieftains to the poorest peasants bringing his measure of grain or lump of butter to the local monastery.[25]

It seems cynical and irreverent to dig out all those base motivations from a sacred doctrine, but without understanding the psychological basis of the doctrine and its strongly implicit appeal to human desires and aspirations, we would not be able to understand how the karmic paradigm worked in Tibet as the central pillar of social order. It is not a pious morality that one can do once a week; it is serious business affecting one's present life as well as future. The method for socialization of compassion (merit-saving activity) therefore uses the same karmic technique. In this sense lamaist moral exhortation goes beyond "Help thy neighbour" type command. Lamas argue that the reason for helping others arises from the belief in rebirth which asserts that since we are all born and reborn in an endless cycle, all beings are related to each other like mother and child. Hence, the rationale for compassion.

> The necessity for helping all other beings is not a gratuitous notion, without valid foundation. Although at present other beings seem unrelated to us, we do in fact have a very close relationship with them, and therefore it is our responsibility to help them. The nature of this bond is that of mother and child. Our present existence is not a self-originated phenomenon but is the product of many former lives.[26]

The author goes on so far as to suggest that when we meditate we should do so with supreme desire to give happiness to all sentient beings. This may not really help beings to overcome their sufferings as such, but will definitely benefit the meditator : "When we look to see if the sentient beings really do have this happiness (that we wished for in our meditation), we find that what we have done in visualization has not affected them directly but has helped us to develop the supreme wish (*i.e.*, resolve)".[27] In Tibet the notion of compassion (*sNyingrje*) was symbolically institutionalized in the person of the ruler, the Dalai Lama who is believed to be the reincarnation of Avlokiteshwara, Buddhistava of Compassion. It is a measure of the deep internalisation of such religious values that many a foreigner was astonished to see how Tibetan children quite consciously avoid killing or harming even insects.[28]

Lest we should be mistaken for romanticizing Tibetan society which was far from being ideal, we should remind ourselves that every act of compassion was considered a definite investment in the interest of the actor. We should also recall that the law of karma stipulates that an action may bear fruit either now in this life or in the next. Further, given two such wide possibilities and also given human nature for what it is, it is not difficult for us to imagine which aspect would be more wished for and correspondingly perhaps emphasized more. One of the more widely held Tibetan beliefs about the law of karma is this : If you do not repay your parents' kindness, the latter part of your life will be a sad one. A common Tibetan proverb establishes a co-relationhip between the purity of mind and the goodness of the universe we live in :

> If (your) mind is pure,
> the earth and skies will be fair too;
> If (your) mind is wicked,
> the earth and skies will be wicked too.[29]

In short, the karmic view of morality is not intrinsic but instrumental. Morality is not good in itself; it is a necessary means to attain one's goal. It is in one's interest, present and future, to act according to the law of karma. It does not seek to scare people but appeals to man's self-interest. Herein lies the secret of its success.

Karma and Ngo-tsa

When religious values are internalized over time, they become functioning social norms as well. Certain actions are considered proper and good not only in the religious sense but also from the point of view of social norms. This is because religion has become the core of shared values and meanings in society. In Tibet "a person who does not recognize karma" (*Las 'Bras La Mi' Zin mKhan Mi*) was considered a bad man by society at large. Thus, karma becomes co-terminous with a purely social norm called *Ngo-tsa*.[30] A sense of shame which is the meaning of *Ngo-tsa* is by no means peculiar to Tibetans; it is a social norm prevalent in most East Asian societies. But in Tibet, children were taught at home and school a keen sense of shame. An American anthropologist, had observed that a "very characteristically Tibetan attitude which this generation (of students) has also acquired in the course of their socialization is a sensitivity to the notion of 'face'".[31]

Ngo-tsa may be considered a social mechanism by which the members of a society are made to conform to certain standards of action and behaviour. Psychologically it is premised on human desire for self-respect, dignity and honour; for the "loss of face" is the negation of self-respect. In this respect it is a reflection of the importance attached to relations between man and man, as opposed to man and things. Tibetans believed that just as a monk cannot continue to live in his monastery if he violated any of his religious vows such as loss of celebacy, a man cannot live in society if he has committed acts which violate the social norm of *Ngo-tsa*. "How can you face others" is a common expression among Tibetans.

Ngo-tsa implies a charge by society at large against a deviant member. What are the acts that would be considered socially "bad" and therefore cases of *Ngo-tsa* ? There is perfect agreement between the law of karma and *Ngo-tsa* in their judgment of what actions and behaviour should be considered bad : killing, stealing, adultery, lying *etc, etc*. Any known case of violation of "The Divine Doctrine of Ten Virtues" (*Lhachos dGe Wa bChu*) and "Human Doctrine of Sixteen Clean Acts" (*Mi Chos rTsangma bChu Drug*)[32] should be a case of both negative karma and *Ngo-tsa*. This is not a mere coincidence to which Tibetans were oblivious. "What sort of man is he who does not recognize the law of karma nor has *Ngo-tsa*?" is another common expression.

Those who were religious might have been more consciously observant of karma and in so doing, they automatically observed *Ngo-tsa* as well. Where the law of karma failed to operate in hopeless cases, *Ngo-tsa* was expected to restrain any anti-social action. *Ngo-tsa* has a practical implication to the deviant's relations with other members of society, which worked as an additional incentive to conform to the social order. If a person committed a particular shameful act of *Ngo-tsa*, he was likely to suffer alienation from society. Perhaps a matter of even greater consequence would be the loss of trust in the "faceless" person. There was no New York, London or Tokyo where one could begin a new life. Both Karma and *Ngo-tsa* assume a face-to-face relationship in a small community where people are few enough to know each other by name and where social mobility is low enough for most people to experience the effects of their asocial actions before too long. This was the case in Tibet.

Karma and social order

I have tried to point out some salient social implications and the psychological basis of karma. We can now look at some of the social functions of karma, and get a glimpse of how value system, action and social structure are inter-related in several ways.

The place of karma within the Buddhist religion as a whole is always defined as the universal law governing all the dynamics of existence, upon whose operation even the Buddha does not have any control. As the core structure of Buddhism, karma provides not only a set of ready-made definitions; it is capable of defining any situation that may arise. Thus, Tibetans could interpret from the Communist takeover of their country to a love affair as a result of karma.[33] Karma gives a general if not universal, definition of the human situation, taking into consideration the past, present and future. It therefore becomes possible for its adherents to define any situation that may arise in karmic terms. Sociologically then, karma provides a universal paradigm of action or event within whose framework it is possible for its adherents to view any particular situation in general karmic terms and define it accordingly. The paradigm works on three principal axes. The actor, situated in the present, acts largely under the karmic forces of his past actions and partly under the circumstances of his present situation which constitutes his freedom of action, to determine his future. Man is invariably placed in a sociological situation; a continuum of social actions and their consequences. Since karma interprets any given situation as a result of some past action(s), it makes it theoretically possible for its adherents to predict the future as well. A Tibetan proverb goes thus : "If you want to find out what you were in your previous life, look at your present status; if you want to know what you would be in your next life, watch your present actions".[34]

One of the fundamental assumptions of the law of karma is a genuine belief in rebirth. In the case of the Buddhist Tibet we may safely accept that assumption as valid. A safety-valve does, however, exist within the theory itself in its ambiguous assertion that an action may produce its results either now in this life or in the next. But deprived of its basic assumption of a life hereafter karma falls on the ground and it is unlikely that its safety-valve will work. Otherwise, karma appears as the precursor of modern religion which "is beginning to understand the laws of the self's own existence and so to help man take responsibility for his own fate".[35] Philosophically, the karmic view of life seems to agree with Joseph Conrad's when he wrote in *Nostromo* : "For life to be large and full it must contain the care of the past and of the future in every passing moment of the present".[36]

The second major social function of karma lies in having created psychological conditions for a stable social order. It obviously tends to legitimatize authority and hierarchy and their obvious concomitant - inequality, as being a result of people's differing past actions. For the lower classes, karma tended to blunt their discontent, resentment, envy and so on, which are generally accentuated by the competitive structure of modern society. Their present low status is karmically interpreted as an inevitable result of a lack of their positive actions in their previous lives.

By distancing and de-personalizing causes of misfortune, karma has the tendency to reduce frustration, anger and the like which generally create friction in social relations. This had some impact on human and social relations in Tibet. An obvious example that tends to substantiate my assertion is the equanimity with which Tibetan refugees face their plight, a fact often noted by foreign visitors.[37]

If we study the implications of karma to class, status and power from the modern perspective, we find that karma is definitely in favour of ruling class and the rich. For the law justifies whatever status one might have in terms of one's past deeds. In this respect karma is a system of transcendental meritocracy, but in actual fact, point out the critics of Tibetan society, karma was used by the ruling class to provide an ideological justification for "serfdom".[38] This may be true to the extent that Tibetans accepted the *status quo* as given (by karma). Tibetans saw the failure of king Mutri Tsanpo's (798-804) three successive attempts at equalization of property between the rich and the poor as vindication of the law of karma.[39]

However, to eqate karma with fatalism is to commit a fundamental mistake. At best this is only half the story in the sense that a person's present status is seen as a function of his past karma. This view omits the other half of the law : one's future—which ambiguously and deliberately includes future here as well as hereafter - will be determined by one's present actions. It is this aspect of karma which provides perhaps the strongest incentive for ethical conduct of social life. Karma provides not only a certain degree of freedom of action but also a high stake in the future for the actor in order to motivate him to do "good" deeds. In other words, the karmic paradigm has two inseparable aspects : an actor is what he is as a result of his past actions and similarly his future will be determined by his present actions. If he continued to live on his past stock, so to speak, he will have not much left for this life and probably none in the next.

Unless we have sufficient evidence to prove that the ruling class did not believe in karma and that only the masses did, we have no way to prove that only the "fatalistic" aspect of karma worked. For the ruling class and the rich it was in their self-interest to do "good deeds" to ensure continued success in life hereafter. In this context I should mention the Tibetan belief that the more generous you are, the richer you would be. This reasoning is obviously based on the logic of karma. Tibetan Buddhist literature is replete with warnings about karmic consequences, especially those directed against the ruling class.

> If you do not take contributions
> Of the wealth obtained from former giving,
> Through your ingratitude and attachment
> You will not obtain wealth in the future.[40]

We have taken some pains to indicate that the reason for believing in karma are very mundane, which partly explains why we have singled out that doctrine as a social ethos determining people's attitude, behaviour and social action. In conclusion, we shall briefly point out the karmic rationale for the general order of existence. The instrumentalist nature of karmic ethos compels members of lamaist society to conform to a certain normative behaviour pattern, more compellingly so than in other religious cases. For the logic of karma runs as follows : If a person commits crime, it is not only sinful in the Juda-Christian theological sense; it is detrimental to one's self-interest which includes here as well as hereafter. If such a largely self-interest motivated observance of social norms is made possible by karma, then the problems of law and order are automatically minimized.[41]

Conforming, therefore, to the religion-ordained social order is not only obeying God's command but definitely acting in one's self-interest. it is then this rational appeal to self-interest and self-responsibility that marks karma not an archaic doctrine but a vital principle of life. It is indeed one of the most modern doctrines that ever evolved out of the Indic religious tradition.

Though religiously conceived, the karmic paradigm has tremendous sociological scope to make good earthy sense of the human condition; it shows a profound understanding of human nature as it is. This implicit mundane aspect of karma, as we have shown, has been accentuated by Buddhist missionaries for instrumental purposes. From the point of view of the original intention of the founder, such excessive emphasis may well represent an unintended digression from the path. But as the Tibetan case illustrates, the theoretical (divine) failure of religion precisely accounts for its practical (sociological) success. Herein lies the historic social function of religion as the inspirer, the idea-giver and above all as the pivot of social order in human society.

We conclude our discussion with a general remark on the comparative study of religion, within whose context we shall try to place karmic ethos. If we compare Max Weber's *The Religion of India*[42] with his better known work *Protestant Ethic and the Spirit of Capitalism* a striking difference becomes apparent. Whereas in the latter he is able to pinpoint a single sect with a revolutionary doctrine, namely Calvinism, Weber seems to be at loss in the former; he is unable to determine or narrow down the cultural factors responsible for the peculiar development in pre-modern India. *The Religion of India* is a general description of Hinduism and Buddhism, based on the then available data in Western languages; its author fails to find the missing link. What was the functional equivalent of Protestant work ethic, that led to the non-capitalist development in Asia? Since all Indic religions—Hinduism, Buddhism, Jainism, Sikhism *etc.*—base some of their major beliefs on the notion of karma, whose sociological significance we have already pointed out, our study[44] suggests that karmic ethos is the functional equivalent, even if negative in its effect in terms of economic rationality, of the Protestant work ethic. It appears that belief in karma among Indians may not be as strong as it is among Tibetans because there is also alternative belief called *Kismat*. Still the belief in karma is deep-rooted among Indians following any of the above-mentioned Indic religions.[45]

Karmic ethos is not characterized by inactivity which the ideal of *yoga* might suggest, as indeed Weber thought when he failed to *single* out any ideas(s) or value(s) from Hinduism or Buddhism with action consequences.[46] As the Tibetan case illustrates, karmic ethos is capable of motivating people into social actions of enormous consequences. To realize this, we have to only recall how Tibetan civilization was built out of the sands and snows of Central Asia.[47] But, of course, it is true that this kind of historical development is different from the early phases of industrial capitalist development in Western Europe. Our point is to question Weber's assertion that the highest ideals of Hinduism (*viz.* yoga *etc.*)[48] necessarily determined the Indian historical development just as the highest doctrines of Christianity (*e.g.* Augustinian philosophy) did not supposedly contribute to the early development of industrial capitalism. Thus, in our paper we have taken ample care to locate not the highest doctrines of Mahayana Buddhism, which we leave to *Geshes;* nor the most important religious ideas, which we leave to the historian of religion. We have spotted a single religious doctrine out of Buddhism (and Hinduism), with action consequences - karma.[49]

Notes and References

1. In comparative perspective, the notion of "face" is not peculiar to only Tibetans. Expressions like losing or saving face are very much current in contemporary speech.
2. David Macdonald, (1926). *The Land of the Lama* (London : Sieley, Service and Co.,) p.59.

3. Ekai Kawaguchi, (1909). *Three Years in Tibet*, (Benares and London : Theosophical Publishing Society) p.549.
4. Zwa-sgab-pa Dban-phyug bde-Idan, (1976). *Bod-kyi-srid-don royal-rabs*. Vols. I and II. (Kalimpong : Shakabpa House) : H.F.Richardson, (1962). *Tibet and its History* (London : Oxford University Press).
5. *The Little Community* (1955). (Chicago : University of Chicago).
6. G.Tucci, (1967). *Tibet Land of Snows* (New York : Stein and Day) p.15.
7. This is the core of the Chinese Communists or their sympathisers' critique of the old social order in Tibet. See *Wrath of the Serfs* (Beijing : Foreign Languages Press, 1976); Anna Lousie Strong, *When Serfs stood up in Tibet* (Beijing : New World Press, 1959).
8. Tsepon W.D.Shakabpa, (1967). *Tibet : A Political History* (New Haven : Yale University Press), p.13.
9. Khache Phalu (1980). *'Jig Rtan Las' Bras rtse-lugs kyi Bslab-Bya Bcas phyogs bsdebs bzhugs-so*. (Dharamsala : Tibetan Cultural Printing Press) pp.46-47.
10. Ta-la'i bLama (xiv),(1963). *Nos kyi yul dan nos kyi mi-man* (Darjeeling:Tibetan Freedom Press) p.40.
11. Ugen Gombo, (1985). "Belief in karma and its social ramifications in Samsara". In Barabara Nimri Aziz and Mathew Kapstein (eds). *Soundings in Tibetan Civilization* (New Delhi: Manohar), pp.237-8.
12. Geshe Rapten. *The Preliminary Traces of Tibetan Buddhism* (Burton, Washington: Tusum Ling Publications), p.19.
13. A much misused term, *bLama* means strictly the Tibetan equivalent of the Sanskrit term Guru. But conventional usage, based on the dominance of lamas in Tibetan Buddhism, means any monk following the Tibetan Buddhist tradition. Our usage of the term "lamaist" also follows this definition of a culture dominated by lamas.
14. To mention a few well known examples : *Sa-skya Legs-bshed Chu-shing bstan-bcos, Bya-sprel Legs-bshed, Dga-ldan legs-shed, Khache Phalu' Namthar Thog-mtha Bar-qsum bsyb-bya etc.*
15. Dawa Norbu, "An Analysis of Sino-Tibetan Relationships 1245-1911". In Aziz and Epstein (eds), *op.cit.*, pp.179-80, 184-85.
16. *Sa-skya-pa'i bka-'bum.* (Tokyo:Tokyo Bunko, 1968) No.210 Ba, pp.147 a-151 a.
17. Nagarjuna and the Seventh Dalai Lama. *The Precious Garland and the Song of the Four Mindfulness*. Translated by Jeffrey Hopkins and Lati Rimpoche, with Anne Klein (London : George Allen and Unwin Ltd., 1975), p.43. This is the present Dalai Lama's selection for the Wisdom of Tibet Series.
18. *Ibid.*, p.19.
19. Stuart and Roma Gelder (1964). *The Timely Rain* (London Hutchinson), p.204.
20. Geshe Rapten, *op.cit.*, p.18.

21. *Ibid.*, p.42.
22. Bstan-'zin rgyaltsan, *Byang-chub sems kyi bstodpa rinchen* sgron-ma. (Varanasi, n.d) p.54.
23. The Dalai Lama, (1962). *My Land and My People* (New York : McGraw Hill), p.61.
24. Heinrich Harrer, (1956) *Seven Years in Tibet* (London : Pan Books).
25. Christoph von Furer-Haimendorf, (1967). *Morals and Merits* (Chicago : University of Chicago Press), p.196.
26. Geshe Rapten, *op.cit.*, p.36.
27. *Ibid.*, p.44.
28. Dervla Murphy, (1970). *The Tibetan Foothold* (London : John Murray).
29. *Sempa dkarma/Sadan nam-yan dkar/Sempa ngan-na/Sa dang nam-yan ngan.*
30. Sarat Chandra Das defines *Ngo tsa* as "shame" in his *A Tibetan-English Dictionary* (Delhi : Motilal Banarsi Dass, 1976),p.356.
31. Margaret Nowak describes in her doctoral dissertation "*Diminal 'Self', Ambiguous 'Power' The Genesis of 'Rangzen' Metaphor Among the Tibetan Youth in India*" (Seattle:University of Washington, 1978) how *Ngo-tsa* technique was used quite publicly to make the failures feel ashamed in front of a whole school assembly in Mussoorie, India, p.66.
32. For a translation of these moral codes, decreed by king Strong-btsan sGam-Bo (d.650 AD) and Khri-Srong/Dev-btsan (b.742), see Franz Michael, *Rule by Incarnation* (Boulder:Westview Press, 1982). Appendix.
33. As the Tibetan expression goes : *Yab-yum skyi-dban btsan-kyan, Las-'gro bkag-nas mi-'thus.*
34. *Snon-ma gan-byas so-so 'lus-la ltos, phyima gan-yon so-so' las-la ltos.*
35. Robert N. Bellah, (1964) "Religious Evolution", *American Sociological Review*, 29, p.372.
36. Cited by Reinhard Bendix (1978). *Kings or Peoples : Power and the Mandate to Rule* (Berkeley & Los Angeles : University of California Press).
37. Han Suyin, (1977). Lhasa, *The Open City* (New York G.P. Putnam's Sons; Ratna Deshapriya Senanayake, *Inside Story of Tibet* (Colombo, Ceylon : Afro-Asian Writers Bureau, 1967).
38. T.C. Palakshappa, (1978). *Tibetans in India* (New Delhi : Sterling). pp.111-113. See also Girija Saklani, (1984) *The uprooted Tibetans in India* (New Delhi : Cosmo).
39. A.H.Francke,. *Antiquities of Indian Tibet* (Archaeological Survey of India, New Imperial Series, 50), p.88.
40. Nagarjuna, *op.cit.* 63.
41. One of the significant exceptions to the rule used to be robbers and highway men who used to rob lonely travellers in remote and isolated places in Tibet.
42. *The Religion of India* (trans.and ed.) by H.H.Gerth and Don Martindale (New York. The Free Press, 1967).

43. *Protestant Ethic and the Spirit of Capitalism* (London : George Allen and Unwin, 1930).
44. This observation is based on the present paper and my unpublished paper "karma and Calvinism:Social Implications of Self-determination and Predestination" presented to Professor Reinhard Bendix `Seminar on Max Weber', (University of California, Berkeley - March 1972).
45. This observation is based on my over two decades of stay in India and contact with Indians.
46. Thus Weber concludes *The Religion of India* as follows: "Asia's partly purely mystical, partly purely innerworldly ascetic goal of self-discipline could take no other form than in emptying of experience of the real forces of experience", p.342.
47. See R.A.Stein, (1972). *Tibetan Civilization* (Stanford : Stanford University) and David Snellgrove and Hugh Richardson, *A Cultural History of Tibet* (New York : Praeger 1968).
48. What Weber called "salvation technology", *op.cit.*, p.166.
49. We have couched the concluding section at such a high pitch that it seems helpful to restrict the applicability of karmic ethos to a more realistic limit. We have used the term "lamaist society" to include not only Tibet but all Tibetan-speaking peoples inhabiting the lamaist culture areas in cis-Himalayan region and Central Asia.

CHAPTER 3

Pre-Buddhistic Rites in Buddhism

Ringu Tulku*

Buddhism is one of the most dominant religions of the Himalaya for more than one millennium now. *Vajrayana,* which accepts the teaching of *Theravada, Mahayana* and *Tantrayana* as a complete teaching of the Buddha, is the Himalayan form of Buddhism. This form of Buddhism which is erroneously called Lamaism, was established in Tibet by Indian saint-scholars like Guru Padmasambhava, Shanta Rakshita, Atish Dipankara and many others, with the help of Tibetan translators and kings. This form of Buddhism is now prevalent throughout the Himalayan ranges.

Before the advent of Buddhism the dominant religion of Tibet was 'Bon'. Bon was so much prevalent in Tibet that some scholars still think that the word 'Bod', which Tibetans call to their land, is a distortion of 'Bon', meaning the land of Bon. The popular appeal of Buddhism soon took over the dominance of Bon. After an open debate between the Buddhist and Bonpo scholars during the reign of king Khrisrong Deutsen (742-798 A.D.), where the Bonpos could not defend their faith, most of the unhealthy and baneful rites and rituals of Bon were abolished. Only a revised form of Bon called the 'White Bon' survived which took in a substantial influence of Buddhism. The oral history of the Tsong people

* Lecturer in Tibetan, Sikkim Government College, Tadong, Sikkim.

in Sikkim say that they are the descendants of those Bonpos who left Tibet around that time. It would make an interesting study to compare the present Bon religion of Tibet with the traditions of the Tsongs.

At the same time Buddhism also accepted some of the unharming and beneficial traditions and rites of Bon and assimilated them into Buddhism. Buddhism is known for its adaptability to its new environments and its ability to assimilate the local traditions without compromising all the same the principles of the doctrine. This brief paper is an endeavour to study how this is done in this particular case.

Before discussing the four popular Bon rites which were adopted by Buddhism and observed by Buddhists throughout the Himalayan belt, it is essential to have a basic structure of Bon religion before us.

'Bon' religion

Bon teachings were first transmitted to the Tibetans by Shenrap Miwo (*bshen-rap-mi-wo-*). Shen means 'heavenly' or 'divine', Rap means 'supreme one' and Miwo means 'great man'. According to the Bonpos, Shenrap lived long before Buddha. The works attributed to Shenrap has a collection of some 400 volumes still preserved. But it is evident that they have undergone heavy editing under the influence of Buddhism.

In contrast to Buddhism—the spirituality of which arises in the far more abstract context of psychology, Bon religion is mainly concerned with the creation of the universe and of the Tibetan people. They pay little heed to the pursuit of salvation through the practice of austerities. Bon aspirants sought magical power through union with the divine nature as manifested in mountains, trees, lakes and rivers—all of which are very impressively present in Tibet. Nine cosmic deities (*Se* and *Degye*) created the world, a world in which birth, death, marriage and sickness all have their place. If the worshipper can attune himself with these gods through various ritualistic ceremonies and through understanding these ceremonies then he is in a position to fulfil whatever is demanded of him by the cosmic order.

The supreme divine principle of the Bon religion is referred to as *Yeshen* (*Ye-gshen*). This supreme deity has the same quality of cosmic totality that is found in most theistic religions. *Ye* means primordial or original and *Shen* means divine, heavenly or spiritual, but also has an anthropomorphic implication. *Yeshen* is seen as passive and peaceful rest for the worshipper.

The energetic aspect of the sphere of the divine is represented by another principle called *Se* (*gsas*). *Se* is primarily vengeful and he communicates directly with man. He creates the link between the absolute divine plane and the relative plane of man. If one could acquire the ability to see the *Yeshen* quality in every life situation then *Se* is a friend. He would then guide the devotee to the appropriate spiritual direction. Otherwise, he, along with *Degye*—the eight cosmos-creating deities—could cause any kind of trouble.

Se sometimes called *Lha* (God) is the chief principle and other *Degyes* are his messengers. To worship *Se* and his messengers are the only way to approach *Yeshen*. Therefore, the different rites and rituals are performed to appease the nine cosmic deities - *Se* and *Degye*. *Degye* might more accurately be regarded as types or principles, than as individual beings, since each may have many local manifestations partaking of its essential character. Each *Degye* also has a retinue of minions, attendants, helpers *etc.* operating on its intentions. *Degye* according to the Bon texts are as follows :

1. Lu (*klu*) : The only female *Degye* Lu is associated with water. She brings rain and fertility. She punishes with leprosy and she is the patron-deity of women.

2. Tsen (*btsan*) : He is the god of fire Associated with speed and accomplishment of actions, especially of instant destruction, he is the patron-deity of bandits and warriors and punishes with heart-attack and accidents.

3. Therong (*the-rangs*) : He is the god of dice. He is the patron-deity of children and blacksmiths and brings success in games and warfare.

4. Dud (*bdud*) : Associated with darkness, he is the god of destruction and brings bad luck.

5. Chuglha (*phyuh-lha*) : He is the god of wealth and the patron-deity of merchants and households. He rewards with prosperity and punishes with poverty.

6. Nyen (*gnyan*) : He is the god of Tibetan folk-culture and patron of rulers and patriots. He is associated with mountains.

7. Za (*gza*) : He is the god of psychological energy, lightening and hailstorms, patron of magicians and associated with dragon. He punishes with epileptic fits and madness.

8. Dralha (*dgra-lha*) : He is the god of war and patron of war lords and warriors.

The term *Degye* appears in many of the Buddhist texts where three and sometimes four categories are mentioned. The Buddhist concept of *Degye* however is totally different. To the Buddhists Degye are *samsaric* beings and objects of sympathy and compassion because they were born in that particular character due to some peculiar *karmic* force. Buddhists do not worship them as the objects of Refuge but they make offerings to them as rewards and presents for not causing harm to people and protecting the good and virtuous.

Lhasang (*Lha-Bsangs*)

The most popular rites of pre-Buddhistic age still observed is *Lhasang* or smoke offerings. In the *Lhasang*, a fire is made of cedar needles and other aromatic woods, and offerings are made of three whites (curd, milk and butter), three sweets (jaguar-brown sugar, crystal sugar and honey), *Tsampa* (flour of roasted barley, staple food of Tibet), beer and tea. This ceremony is usually performed on the highest peak in the locality. The cedar is believed to be the tree of *Se* and its smoke is believed to bring the divine down into the sphere of human life and to elevate the performers into the sphere of divine. Therefore, this ceremony purifies and energises the positive powers of the event or the individuals for whom it is performed. The performers get absorbed themselves in the smoke, go round the fire and shout *ki-ki-so-so-Lha-gyal-lo* (may god be the victorious). Certain messages are read in the pattern of the smoke. To give an example, a gentle rising white smoke signifies acceptance while dark smoke constantly interrupted by wind signifies obstacles.

In the Buddhist *Lhasang*, offerings are made to the Buddhas and Buddhist pantheon of deities, lamas of different lineages, the *Dharmapalas* and also *Degye* and six realms of the world. The most significant change in all the pre-Buddhistic rites performed by the Buddhists is that they are performed in the Buddhist way, *i.e.*, beginning with Refuge prayer and *Bodhisattva* vow and ending with dedicating the merits for the sentient beings. The *Lhasang* is performed on all auspicious occasions like welcoming a dignitary and to honouring a departed soul. The ceremony is always performed in the morning and the best time would be the sunrise.

Lalhu (*bla-bslu*)

Another important rite which is brought down from the Bon tradition is *Lalhu* meaning ransoming of *La*. The concept of *La* is somewhat similar to soul. It is believed that a man needs three things to keep alive, *i.e.*, *La* - the soul, *Tshe* - longevity of life and *srof* - living force. In the Bon belief, animals do not possess a *La*. The *La* is a part of one's being but it can be stolen, confiscated, or regained, as well as reinforced by spiritual power. When the *La* of a person leaves him, his vigour and health deteriorates and if not revived the man becomes ill and finally dies.

Lalhu ceremony is performed partly to give a ransom to the confiscator of the *La*, and partly to remagnetize the *La* to the sick person. It is also performed to stabilise the *La* of a new born baby. The ceremony includes reconsecration of *La-yu (ble-gyu) La* turquoise stone, *La-phor (bla-phor) La cup*, and *La-lug (bla-lug) La* sheep. On the final day of the *Lalhu* ceremony a figure of a sheep is made of butter with *Layu* inside it and placed inside the *La-phor*. *La-phor* is then made to revolve in a basin full of water. Messages are read from this ceremony as to whether the *La* has returned or not.

Buddhists perform the *Lalhu* ceremony either with a *Tshe-drup* (*tshe-sgrub*) - Long life practice, or along with the worship of a long-life deity like Amitayus or White Tara.

Toh (*gto*)

Toh is another category of pre-Buddhistic rites which has got an astrological background as well. According to Buddhist mythology, it was preached by Manjushri in China as a part of astrology. The rite, along with Chinese astrology (*Wag-tsi*) spread in Tibet through kong-tse Khrul-gyi Gyalpo. It probably became a part of the Bon rites before the advent of Buddhism in Tibet because *Toh* was a rite widely practised by the Bonpos. Buddhism later assimilated the rites giving it a Buddhist flavour.

Toh is a group of rites designed to achieve great results by employing simple and sometimes idiotic methods. Some simple ceremonies consist of just throwing sheep droppings into the river while difficult ones require licking of red hot iron by the performer.

There are *Toh* methods to solve almost every human problem right from warding off the bad stars to the extent of birth control measures. *Toh* methods are grouped into two categories; one to bring benefits and another to bring harm. Buddhists refrain from practising the second category.

Doo (*mdos*)

The *Doo* ceremony is performed to appease different *Degyes* and their retinue. This ceremony in the original Bon required the sacrifice of animals which were later substituted with figures of animals made of dough or mud.

In this ceremony the *Degye* is offered a new castle, a very elaborate but miniature construction called *Doo*. The remnants of *Doo* consisting of lots of figures made of mud or dough and a colourful structure fashioned out of thread and bamboo is a common site on the road sides of the hill stations of the Himalaya. With the help of *mantra* and meditative power of the performer this structure is magnified into a heavenly abode abounding in all the luxuries of the world. Since everything that *Degye* would want would be available in this new castle created by meditation, *mantra* and materials the intent of this rite would be to lure the particular *Degye* into the *Doo* —not only out of the sick person but also out of his own dwelling place and bid him never to harm anybody.

In these four categories of rites are included almost all the pre-Buddhistic rites of Tibet adopted by Buddhism. As mentioned earlier, many changes have taken place in these rites—changes not in their basic structure, but in the concept, purpose and philosophy behind them. This, I think, is true in all the cases of adaptation Buddhism has made throughout its long course of history.

Notes and References

1. *Works of Ju Mipham*, Vol. Dhi.
2. Chogyam Trungpa Rinpoche. "The Bon Way of Life", *Vajradhatu* Vol. 7, No.2.

CHAPTER 4

Social Adaptation of Buddhism in Indian Himalayas : Contemporary Processes

Bina Roy Burman*

The Himalayan region of India extends from Kashmir on the west to the easternmost tip of Arunachal Pradesh. Historically speaking, due mainly to the encouragement Buddhism received in the hands of emperor Asoka and in the hands of some of the Greek rulers, it spread to Afghanistan and beyond Central Asia. During the reign of the Kushan dynasty it received protection in the trans-Himalayan regions and spread to Central Asia. Though Buddhism originated in India, it attained its distinct flavour in western and central Himalaya, where the *Mahayana* Buddhism struck its roots. At a later stage the different sects evolved in Tibet and these sects of the *Mahayana* Buddhism spread in some of the areas of the Indian Himalayan region. This is considered to be an adaptation to the geographical situation, to segmental character of the society resulting from diversities of terrain and to the ethnocultural differentiations prevailing in the region.

---

* Post-Doctoral Fellow, ICSSR, New Delhi.

In the western Himalayan regions like Kashmir, Ladakh, Lahaul and Spiti, Buddhism retained its influence for several centuries. Except in Kashmir, it still has influence on the population of the other areas. It is believed that Guru Padmasambhava was born in Udayana, adjacent to Kashmir, and that he had spent some time in Kashmir.[1] Tilopa hailed from western Himalayan region. The king priest Yeshe Od too did his best to spread Buddhism in these areas. In keeping with these traditions we find that the present-day Ladakh has the living tradition of the *Mahayana* Buddhism and has monasteries of almost all the sects of Buddhism.

Kashmir was a Buddhist region but it is not so today while Buddhism has survived in Ladakh due to the enthusiasm and interest shown by the people there. Ladakh also came under the cultural influence of Muslim Kashmir and Mughal empire but the religious life there continued to be of the same traditional pattern and there was no deviation. Till this century, in Ladakh, we find the monasteries functioning in the traditional ways. After the entrance of Islam to Kashmir, Ladakh turned increasingly eastward, to Tibet, and the cultural bridge was maintained till the occupation of Tibet. Thus, the monastery of Lamayaru belongs to the *Bri-gung-pa* sect, (a branch of the *Kagyudpas*).[2] As we know, this order took its birth from the original teachings of the two famous Indian scholars, Naro-pa and Tilo-pa, and Marpa received these traditions of *Mahamudra* from them.

The other *Bri-gung-pa* monastery is Phyapbang, founded by king Tashi Namgyal. The monastery of Maungya belongs to the *Nying-Ma-pa* (*rNying-ma-pa*) sect[3] and the monastery of Likir belongs to the *Gulugpa* (*dGe-lugs-pa*) sect. After the conversion of Kashmir to Islam new monasteries grew in Ladakh *e.g.* Spituk, Likir (*Gelugpa*) and Tiktse. In Ladakh the Kagyudpa sect has exercised great influence. Both the *Bri-gung-pa* and *Brug-pa* branches established monasteries there—which persist till the modern era. The Hemis monastery is the foremost among the *Brug-pa* monasteries. The *Sa-skya-pa* sect has Ma-to monastery and the *Nying-Ma-pas* have Tra-tok monastery.[4]

Thus practically, all sects of Tibetan Buddhism are represented till to-day. After the demise of the royal patron in Ladakh all the monasteries became quite independent. But as the present author had found in her earlier studies, the members of different sects are generally not united, and sectarian factionalism has continued through the centuries. The same condition prevails in Ladakh as well.

After the Chinese annexation of Tibet the cultural contact with Tibet has almost ceased completely. The chief abbot of Hemis was discovered in Tibet, but he could not return to Ladakh from Tibet, where he had gone to study, due to Chinese occupation.[5] No new incarnation could be found as his replacement as it would go against the Tibetan Buddhist religious norms and practices. There was a settlement of the Ladakhi community in Lhasa, the capital of Tibet.[6] There they felt quite at home due to similarity in cultral life and ethnic background. Apart from this, a regular trade-route was used by Ladakhis to Lhasa, and they depended to a great extent on this trade-route as well as on the northern trade-route to Kashgar. But due to Chinese interference both the trade-routes have been closed to the Ladakhis.

In addition to the disruption in cultural link, there has been a major change in the economic life of the Ladakhis of both the societies, the lay as well as monastic. As trade has always been a source of income to the members of monastic society—even as a corporate body—this loss was too great for the people of this region. Moreover the objects which were admired as symbols of their culture by the Ladakhi society are no longer available to them.

Ladakhi is the spoken language in the Ladakh region while the script is Tibetan. But during the last few decades distinctiveness of Ladakhi dialect is being emphasized even in written form with the obvious encouragement of the Government of India. This seems to be an adaptation to the political context. Tibetan can be taken as an optional subject in government schools.[7] A Buddhist Philosophical School has been established at Choklamsar near Leh. The intention is to educate the young monks in Tibetan, Sanskrit and Buddhist philosophy and English. Unfortunately this Institute has not been able to satisfy the need of higher standard of education, as expected by the scholarly lamas.[8]

The agricultural work in Ladakh is carried out in traditional style, the crops being barley, wheat and oats. Though irrigation is practised, sufficient food is not produced. About 2000 Tibetan refugees have been settled in Ladakh and they have a carpet weaving centre. It seems that the Ladakhi people are keen to take the opportunities of employment which army and the civil administration offer. But the traditional economic pattern has been greatly disturbed. Naturally the social pattern too will be influenced by it. If the traditionl religious life is to survive, the people of Ladakh must be dynamic. To some extent, the trend is visible. The Buddhists of Ladakh visit Dharamsala as it is the present abode of the Dalai Lama, and for *Gelugpas*, it is definitely a source of inspiration. (For others too he holds the topmost position in the Buddhist hierarchy in the new emerging context.) They must try new avenues of production and trade so that their socioeconomic, religious and cultural life can survive and can make progress. The Buddhist culture and philosophy with an ethical bias had created a particular blend of civilised society in Asia, and the Ladakhis will be able to continue with their way of life with some effort and dynamism.

Influence of the Mahayana Buddhism is still present in the Lahaul and Spiti districts of the western Himalaya. The Lahaul *tehsil* has more Hindu population and Spiti *tehsil* is a Buddhist majority area. Due to the geophysical condition population is thin. Even then, Spiti has several monasteries and Buddhism is a living religion here. Francke had discovered frescoes, which were executed by Indian Buddhist monks who might have taken shelter in the Himalayan region during the early Islamic attacks.[9] At the same time the name of Rinchen Zangpo, the famous scholar and translator is associated with many monasteries of this region. He had translated the *Prajnaparamita* and had distributed the copies to all the monasteries founded by him. The king turned-into-priest Yesha Od had built the Toling monastery, and Rinchen Zangpo was the abbot of the monastery in the Ngari state of Tibet.[10] On his way to Tibet the great scholar Atish too halted at this monastery. These areas are adjacent to both Ladakh and Spiti. Hence direct cultural influence of this region was great both on Ladakh and Spiti. Due to the geophysical nature of the region and the continuous trade relationhip through the important land routes, this influence was strong and continuous. Here it is to be noted that in general Buddhism has been associated to a great extent with trade-routes and merchants in all Buddhist countries in the past, including India.

With such cultural heritage Spiti is proud of the ancient and more or less recent monasteries like *Gelugpa* monastery at Tabo (probably built by the king of Ladakh).[11] The kyi or ki monastery was probably built by Brom-ston, the pupil of Atish in the 11th century.[12] Ki and Drangkhar monasteries belong to the Gelugpas. The Pyin monastery belongs to the *Nyingmapa* (*nNying-Ma-pa*) sect, and the Kaze monastery belongs to the *Sakyapa* (*Sa-skya-pa*) sect. Except Pyin monastery, the other monasteries used to maintain contact and intercourse with the Tibetan monasteries, and they did not differ from them.

In the modern era, education is no longer a monopoly of the monastic establishments, and secular education is being imparted by the government and other bodies. Education is imparted in Tibetan language. The District Census Handbook says regarding cultural activities. "In the past monasteries used to be centres of religious and cultural activities but with the passage of time these activities appear to be on the wane. The lamas still teach dramatics, painting and sculpture in the monasteries throughout the length and breadth of the district."[13] At the instance of the Block authorities twelve *bhajan* and *kirtan mandalis*, ten *mahila samitis* and two *balwari* centres have been established.[14]

Is the government or the local authority unwilling to encourage the Buddhist monastic cultural activities which are generally quite sophisticated? Does it want to encourage the Hindu religious organisations like *Kirtan, bhajan mandalis* and welfare activities by women organisations, creches and *balwaris*? Secular education is being encouraged and all school going students get stipends. With the emphasis on secular activities and organisations with the closing of the Indo-Tibetan border the religious life has to take a different turn.

Though Ladakh, Lahaul and Spiti in the west, and Darjeeling, Sikkim, Arunachal Pradesh in the east came under the religio-cultural orbit of Mahayana Buddhism, the centres of their normative control were in Tibet. With the political merger of Tibet with China a sharp break of the geographical locale of the traditional network has taken place. The Dalai Lama and many heads of important monasteries and sects have taken refuge in India. While the Dalai Lama has established his headquarters at Dharamsala in Himachal Pradesh, some of the important monasteries of the *Gelugpa* sect have established their centres in Karnataka.

The *Nyingmapa* sect has two important centres in South India, a few in Himachal Pradesh, and a few scattered in the eastern Himalayas near Darjeeling. Though the number is about thirtyfive, only a few have reasonable number of monks.

The *Gelugpa* sect has been able to establish itself in a stronger way : Ganden with two colleges, Drepung with two colleges in north and south Karnataka and in Arunachal, and the Tawang monastery was already functioning. The present author had the opportunity to observe the day-to-day functioning of the Sera monastery for about twenty days, and in Ganden Drepung complex for about a week. These well-established monasteries are maintaining their traditions, as well as adapting to the new situations arising out of a change in the total context.

The lower tantric college has been established at Hunsur, Gurupara in Karnataka, and the Gyud-Tyo Tantric University in Bomdila, in Arunachal. Apart from these institutions various small centres and monasteries are scattered in the western and eastern Himalayan areas and some have been established in the settlements, at Bodh Gaya, Sarnath and Varanasi.

The *Kargyudpas* (*bka-brGyud-Pas*) have two bigger monasteries in Rumtek, Sikkim and in Darjeeling with 222 and 130 monks respectively. The *Sakyas* and the *Kar-ma-pas* (*bkar-Ma-pas*) too have their monasteries. A few of them are situated in the western Himalayan region, while some are in the settlements of south India. There are also a few near Darjeeling in West Bengal. During a recent visit to some of the *Sakya* and *Nyingma* monasteries, the present author felt that their organisation was a little loose and that the standard of education and discipline was somewhat inadequate in comparison with the bigger monasteries of the *Gelugpa* sect.

In the changed context, several cross currents are noticeable in the organisational structure, theological formulation, normative aspects of day-to-day life and their world-view. Being uprooted from their age-old milieu the followers of all the sects of the *Mahayana* Buddhism are evincing both centripetal and centrifugal tendencies.

In Dharamsala the Dalai Lama is always there to give inspiration and guidance to the monasteries there and elsewhere. Both lay and monastic organisations have established connection with the centre at Dharamsala. Though the Namgyal Monastery is a small one, it draws monks even from remote Arunachal, and has been a source of inspiration to all Gelugpa monks in India. Even the *Karmapa, Sakyapa* and *Nyingmapa* Buddhists visit Dharamsala to pay their homage to the Dalai Lama.

At the time of *Losar*, *Monlam* (the great prayer) in 1975 the present author found that a large number of monks and abbots joined the religious rites at Dharamsala. The members of the other sects have an ambivalent attitude towards the Dalai Lama and the establishment associated with him. The important monks of various sects are in a way competing with each other for expansion and progress of their sects. They have established monasteries or centres abroad in European countries as well as in Canada and the United States of America many of which are doing well. Still, the Dalai Lama is looked upon as a symbol of the *Mahayana* Buddhism.

In November 1960, a meeting of the heads and prominent lamas of various sects with the Dalai Lama was held at Dharamsala, and a resolution was passed on inter-sectoral harmony.[15] Introspection has started among the Tibetans and it has been pointed out that religion is the cause of disunity among them. But at the same time there is a conscious effort to accept the leadership of the Dalai Lama and to merge the differences. The monk scholars and others have also begun to analytically examine the contents, norms and roles of the different sects.[16]

Under the leadership of the Dalai Lama the monastic system of education has been supplemented with new subjects like English language and History of Tibet. In some of the monastic establishments they have been able to introduce the new subjects.

New centres of advanced studies in Tibetan language and philosophy have also come up. The Tawang monastery of Arunachal belongs to the *Gelugpa* sect. It was affiliated to the Drepung monastery of Tibet. After the Tibetan refugees were settled in Bomdila, the new advanced Tantric college has been established. The Central Institute of Higher Tibetan Studies at Varanasi is another example of his dynamism.

In the traditional system not much emphasis was placed on writing. The method of examinations followed was debate. Though efficient translators and copyists were there, very few Tibetans wrote in general. The Dalai Lama has introduced written examinations in the monasteries and consequently writing has received more attention. He has blended the modern trends with the traditional.

The leadership has accepted modern norms in various walks of life. The Tibetan Children's Village has been established at Dharamsala.

Numerous central schools have been established in the settlements for imparting secular education. Education is no longer a monopoly of the monastic establishments. The leadership is encouraging the people to accept modern system of medicine along with the traditional. Earlier, medicine was connected with astrology and magical rites in addition to medicine.

The modern economic organisations like co-operatives are being run in the lay Tibetan society as well as in the monastic establishments, like Ganden, Sera and Drepung. Several handicraft centres which are mostly co-operative organisations concerned with making carpets are able to sell them in the internal market as well as to export them.

Thus we find that the Tibetans are now organised both in the lay and monastic societies. The Lama Co-operative at Sera uses tractors and jeeps, run a dairy and markets the agricultural, dairy and textile products. The cooperative has come up so well that at times it takes on lease the lands of local residents for agricultural purposes.

The adaptability in the new situation has been possible because of the dynamic leadership from Dharamsala and the modern outlook of the Dalai Lama himself. An understanding and positive attitude of the Government of India has also been instrumental in this regard.

The Dalai Lama's position as the religious head of the *Gelugpa* sect and as the political head of the Tibetans has undergone a change. Apart from being the religious head of a sect, he is being looked upon as a source of legitimisation of the changes in the normative aspects of social and cultural adaptations that are taking place in the new context.

This development represents a continuity with the past as well as an opportunity for incorporation of the new.

Among other cross currents, mention is to be made of the fact that the different areas of the Indian Himalaya are today having direct contact with the centres of Buddhist learning and socialisation such as Bodh Gaya, Nalanda and so on. Some centres have come up in these regions also. Again, the submerged local socio-cultural and linguistic identity are asserting themselves. Simultaneously through printed literature and mass media, they are making parallel attempts to give definite shape to the ecumenical trends in Buddhism compatible with the ideological and humanist challenges of modern times.

Notes and References

1. A.H.Francke, (1972). *Antiquities of Indian Tibet,* Vol.I, (New Delhi: S.Chand & Co.,) p.109.
2. David Snellgrove and Tadensz Skorupski, (1977). *The Cultural Heritage of Ladakh* (New Delhi: Vikas), pp.17-18.
3. *Ibid.*, p.22.
4. *Ibid.*, p.132.
5. *Ibid.*, p.127.
6. Charles Bell, (1968).*Tibet, Past and Present* (Oxford: Univ.Press), p.180.
7. Snellgrove and Skorupski, *op cit.*, 1977,p.140.
8. Reported verbally by an eminent Indian sociologist, who was approached by the monks.
9. Francke, *op.cit.*, p.40.
10. W.D.Shakabpa, (1967). *Tibet : A Political History* (Yale:University Press), p.58.
11. Francke, *op.cit.*, p.41.
12. *Ibid.*, p.45.
13. *District Census Handbook, Lahaul and Spiti* (1968), Government of Punjab, p.30.
14. *Ibid.*, p.30.
15. *Tibetan Review*, Sept., 1976, p.20.
16. *Tibetan Review*, Sept., 1976, several articles.

CHAPTER 5

Sikkimese Buddhism in the Nineteenth Century

Trevor Ling*

Persistence of the marks of urban origin

The characteristic nature of Buddhism in Sikkim is best understood when it is related to the nature of the Buddhist presence in Tibet from the seventeenth century onwards. The basically urban character of Tibetan Buddhism is seen in the concentration of religious professionals in large monasteries (which were virtually colleges) and in its association with books, a script, and a complex social organization. 'What civilization and literature the Sikkimese now possess they owe to Lamaism', observed Austine Waddell.[1] On the other hand, the pre-Buddhist forms of religion in Sikkim, which exist side by side with Buddhist rituals and organizations, accord well with Weber's characterization of the religiosity of peasants : 'a compelling sorcery directed against spirits who rule over or through natural forces ... orgiastic and ecstatic states of "possession", produced by means of toxics or the dance....'[2] These are precisely the features described by Geoffrey Gorer in his account of Mun religious practice in Sikkim : 'priests are simply individuals who, through their possession by a spirit, have certain gifts and duties'. He mentions also those who 'dance until the supernatural speaks through them and discloses its wants and whereabouts'. They make sacrifices of

* Professor of Sociology, Singapore National University, Singapore.

animals of various kinds, such as ox, pig and chicken to devils and other supernatural beings, not only with exorcism in view, but for various other purposes also. And they do so on an individualistic basis rather than as members of an organized order.[3]

Sikkimese Buddhism, on the other hand, still bears the marks of a basically urban character : there are no animal sacrifices. The foundation and justification of Sikkimese Buddhism are contained in its 'two enormous collections of holy writings, the *Kangyour* or commandments ... and the *Tangyour* or commentaries', in the reading of which is found all knowledge necessary for the conduct of life, and the reading of which is the 'essential preliminary to acquiring merit', comments Gorer.[4]

As in Tibet, so also in Sikkim, education is associated with Buddhism, and particularly with the life of the religious profession. The latter is set within the framework of a sophisticated social organization which has its hierarchy of monastic grades : *chapti-bu* or novice; *Tongpeun-bu* and *kane*, (minor monastery officials) *chene*, and *chitembu* (career grades), *chichembu*, *omzet*, and *Dorje Lapoon*, the latter two comprising the highest ranks. It is this disciplined social organization which is the most alien element in the rural life of Sikkim, but it has been maintained largely by reason of the strong links with the monasteries of Tibet. As Gorer comments, 'in so far as they have accepted the social organization of lamaism, the Lepchas have incorporated a new and alien element in their lives.'[5] In this way, with its antipathy to animal sacrifices, its emphasis upon book-learning, and its disciplined social organization, the Tibetan Buddhist presence in Sikkim retains the marks of a distant urban origin.

Until 1975 there was a sense in which Sikkim was still a Buddhist state, although its links with Tibet had been snapped from about 1950 when the Tibetan uprising against the Chinese invasion took place. Sikkim under the Chogyals, like Tibet under the Dalai Lamas, has been described at various times as feudalistic and oppressive. However, the Buddhist state of Sikkim was one in which the majority of the Hindu immigrants from Nepal found it easier to make a living than in their native Nepal, practically the last surviving Hindu state. This suggests that the political and economic advantages of having rulers who are of one's own 'world religion' are fairly slight compared with the advantages of a benign economic system. This was a view by no means unknown among the early Buddhists of India.[6] As Weber recognized, it is the economic cosmos determining more than is commonly admitted by the pious.

However, cut off now from its original urban base in Tibet, and incorporated into the secular (although still in some senses predominantly Hindu) state of India, surrounded by a still deeply rural culture, the Buddhist presence in Sikkim, in term of the theory put forward here, cannot with any certainty be regarded as likely to ensure. But it has to be remembered that in terms of a multifactorial theory of change the critical factor in one historical situation may lose that critical role in another situation at some later time. Thus, the critical factor in the persistence of Buddhism, namely the preservation of its urban character or at least a strong link with an urban base, may in conjunction with the rise of other new and important factors lose something of its critical role.

The nature of the new factors which could affect the continuance of the Buddhist presence in Sikkim cannot yet be clearly identified, in the absence of sufficient empirical data. However, the Darjeeling District of West Bengal, adjoining Sikkim's southern frontier, has been exposed to a greater variety of social interaction and change than Sikkim, and may provide some pointers.

In any case, the need for re-orientation has been experienced at previous times in Sikkim's history. To recall some of the circumstances of previous reorientation may help to provide a basis for assessing the likelihood of another successful re-orientation in obedience to Buddhism's basic urban character.

The Re-orientation of Sikkimese Buddhism in the nineteenth century

There was a rapid and remarkable growth in the number of Buddhist *gumpas* in Sikkim betweeen 1840 and 1860. The distribution of the *gumpas* of Sikkim before that time was as follows :[7]

Table 1

The Distribution of Gumpas and their years of establishment in Sikkim

	Names of Gumpas	*Founded in*
Western Sikkim :	Sanga Chelling	1697
	Dubdi	1701
	Pemayangtse	1705
	Senan	1716
	Tashiding	1716
	Rinchinpong	1730
	Ralong	1730
	Mali	1740
	Katsuperri	1788
Eastern Sikkim :	Gangtok	1716
	Rumtek	1740
	Phodang	1740
Northern Sikkim :	Lachung Tangmoche	1788
	Chuntang	1788
	Talung	1789
	TOTAL : 15	

It will be noticed that the area in which Buddhism was the strongest was the western part of Sikkim where, by 1740, there were eight *gumpas*, all within a radius of about seven miles. During the middle years of the eighteenth century there were three *gumpas* in eastern Sikkim, again within a radius of about seven miles. In the penultimate decade of the eighteenth century came the three *gumpas* in the northern part of the country. The oldest *gumpa*, Sanga Chelling (1697), is in the farthest west. The second oldest is also one in the extreme west, namely Dubdi (1701), in what Hooker described as 'the earliest civilized corner of Sikkim'.[8] Whether Hooker intended it so or not the word 'civilized' has a double significance. It could mean that a civilized place was the appropriate place to found a *gumpa,* or that, a *gumpa* having been founded, it naturally became a civilized place. Either way there is a connection between a 'civilized' or, in certain respects 'urban' place and the presence of a *gumpa.* This was the extent of Buddhist 'civilization' in Sikkim in the eighteenth century.

The first *gumpa* to be built in the nineteenth century was Namchi, in the south-west, in 1836. Then from 1840 until 1860 came a period of great activity in the building of new *gumpas.* In those twenty years fourteen new *gumpas* came up. All but two of these, at Dalling and Yangong, were in the east or the north of the country. Dalling and Yangong are in the central area between the Great Rangeet and the Tista rivers, to the east of the original 'civilized' heartland.

Until 1775, the Raja of Sikkim's domain extended westward as far as Hedanga on the River Arun. It seems that he required the people in that area 'to build *chorten* and *mani* walls in lieu of revenue'.[9] But this control of the western terrain by Sikkim ended in 1775 when the Gorkha rulers, possibly with encouragement from the Bhutanese, conquered the whole area from the position they then held in the extreme east of Nepal, eastwards again as far as the present border between Nepal and Sikkim. Thirteen years later, in 1788, the Gorkhas advanced even farther east into present-day Sikkimese territory, and in that year the whole of West Sikkim as far as the Tista was overrun and occupied by the Gorkha forces.

At that time (in 1788) there were in Sikkim fourteen *gumpas,* according to the list given by Waddell, including Khechuperi, which was founded in 1788. In 1814 the capital of Sikkim, which had been at Rabdentse, was moved to the east, to Tumlong, where it would be less in danger from the Nepalese side. *Gumpa* building had virtually come to an end in West Sikkim.[10] This is in striking contrast to the frequency of the building of new *gumpas* in West Sikkim before 1788 (eight in ninety years); in the next hundred years only one was built in that area. This change of pace is capable of more than one explanation. For example, the area might have by 1788 reached the point of saturation in terms of need, or capacity to support further *gumpas.* However, this explanation is not very impressive, for it seems that the number of *gumpas* and lamas did not keep up with the natural increase of the Bhutia and Lepcha communities.[11]

The explanation may well lie elsewhere. Even after 1817, when the Treaty of Titalia had restored to the Raja of Sikkim his sovereignty over the area east of the Mechi river and west of the Tista (which had been occupied by the Gorkhas) the capital of Sikkim remained in Tumlong, in the east of the country, where it had been established three years before. Moreover, it was in this area, around Tumlong (within a radius of ten miles) that six new *gumpas* were constructed in the next five decades, *gumpas* which had a total capacity for over two hundred lamas.

New *gumpas* continued to be founded, in the east mostly but also in the north, in the areas of the upper Tista valley, near to the line of the trade route northwards through the Kangra La into Tibet.

On the basis of the figures furnished by Waddel in 1894 for the number of lamas in each *gumpa*, the following table, in which *gumpas* are allocated to regions of Sikkim, indicates the growth in numbers of lamas in the different regions between 1720 and 1890 :

Table 2

No. of Lamas in Sikkim

Year	*West*	*East*	*North*	*South*	*Total*
1720	191	3	-		194
1730	206	3	-	80	289
1740	221	183	-	80	484
1790	232	183	103	80	598
		(Rise of Gorkha Power, 1775f.)			
1840	232	318	103	80	733
1850	232	378	111	104	825
1860	232	428	147	104	911
1880	237	448	147	104	936

Thus, in percentage terms, in 1720 the West Sikkim contained 98 per cent of the lamas and the East only 2 per cent. But by 1880 the West had only 25 per cent, while the East had 48 per cent, the North 16 per cent, and the

South 11 per cent. That is to say, in about a century and a half the Buddhist presence in Sikkim had undergone an important geographical shift. After the rise of the Gorkha power, the West appears to have remained static in terms of places available for lamas. Figures given by Percy Brown for 1944 indicate that the whole cluster of ten *gumpas* in West Sikkim (Sanga Chelling, Pemayangtse, Katsuperri, Dubdi, Mali, Rinchingpong, Tashiding, Senan, Ralong and Dolling) had increased their number of lamas by 78 in the period of fifty years since Waddell's report in 1894. But in only five *gumpas* in the East Sikkim in the same period (Gangtok, Rumtek, Phodang, Phensung and Kartok) the increase had been 156. That is to say, the growth still continued at a more rapid pace in the East.

A significant fact is that in the new round of *gumpa*-building that followed that most aggressive period of Gorkha expansion (roughly between 1840 and 1860) the new *gumpas* were located in the Tista valley region, that is, in the eastern half of the country. The choice of sites was, from that time, limited to the present extent of the state of Sikkim, for what now forms the Darjeeling District of West Bengal had in 1835 been ceded to the East India Company, and with it, within its boundaries, a Sikkimese *gumpa,* Bhutia *Basti,* which is now on the outskirts of Darjeeling town. This was a branch of Phodang, and the branch had maintained its link with its parent *gumpa* until the present time, even though it is no longer in the state of Sikkim. (This *gumpa* was destroyed by the Gorkhas in 1786-89 and was later shifted to Mahakal Danra. Eds.) The principle of dependency of smaller and newer *gumpas* upon larger and older ones is a regular feature of Tibetan Buddhist organization. In Sikkim the arrangement before the Chinese occupation of Tibet was that smaller monasteries would be dependent on Pemayangtse, for example, and Pemayangtse in turn would be dependent on, or linked institutionally with Mindolling in central Tibet. The principle can be traced back to the early days of Buddhist institutions in India, when the primary centres were in urban places and were the source of strength for smaller centres established in rural places, with the result in some cases, as the present writer has suggested elsewhere, that when the urban Buddhist communities disappeared so also did the smaller rural ones before long.[12] This principle is obviously one of importance in the present period of change and upheaval in Sikkim, as it is also, perhaps to a lesser extent, in neighbouring Bhutan. But during the period in Sikkim with which we are here concerned, when this small country had a potentially troublesome and disruptive neighbour to the West and a friendly and at that time powerful ally to the North, it is understandable that it was in those areas that gave best access and communication with Tibet that the Buddhist community tended to expand.

Relations between Tibet and Sikkim during the nineteenth century may be seen as an illustration of this principle at work. In the Tibetan case there is an added dimension, not present in the earlier Indian examples : the lamas were the guardians of Buddhist traditions and lineages, and there were also the political rulers. Because of this the assistance given by Tibet to what in some respects might be called its southern extension, that is, Sikkim, is seen by many commentators as part of the political power game in the eastern Himalaya in the nineteenth century. No doubt in certain respects it was, but in this particular case it was more than that. Physical access to Tibet was an important factor in Sikkim's existence and survival as an arena of Buddhist religion and culture. It was this same relative ease of access as attracted the attention of East India Company, keen for trade with Tibet and also the attention of the British government once the tea gardens in Darjeeling District were beginning to be productive. Hence, the well-known result : that the British, wishing to protect this route for their own purposes, had a strong interest in resisting Gorkha expansion eastwards along the Himalayan foot-hills. These things are mentioned because the geography of travel was evidently, at that stage of history an important matter for the Buddhist lamas in Sikkim; especially important was travel with least difficulty to Tibet and their urban centres there.

Thus, since the capital of Sikkim was shifted Tumlong, in 1814, the centre of gravity of Sikkimese affairs moved eastwards, nearer to the routes which led to Tibet, either by way of Kangra or by Chumbi valley, and thus farther away from the troubled western frontier area bordering the kingdom of Nepal. A cluster of *gumpas* grew up around Gangtok (Enchay, Kartok, Simik, Pabia) near the trade route at Phensang and Labrang, Ringyoun and Gyaton, and at Lachen.

Thus the Buddhist community in Sikkim, responding to new geopolitical pressures and processes, was reoriented from its eighteenth century pattern of distribution to a nineteenth century one which, in its turn, has been followed by yet another from the middle of the twentieth century.

It is clear that changes of an even more drastic nature have occurred during the present century, especially since the independence of India in 1947 from the British rule, but above all since the Chinese take-over in Tibet in 1959. The transformation of Sikkim's northern and eastern borders into international frontiers with China began what may now perhaps be seen as the complete turn-about in the outward perspective of Sikkim from 1959 onwards. No longer, it seemed, could the monasteries of Sikkim look northwards for communication with the monasteries of Tibet, and for help and support of other kinds from that direction. This, and the growth within India of colonies of Tibetan refugees, in the western Himalayas, in south India, and, especially, in Darjeeling and Kalimpong, required a re-orientation of a fairly drastic kind. There is no reason to suppose that Sikkim's Buddhists are now to be regarded as part of a dying species, however. The history of the Jews since the overthrow of Jerusalem by the Roman Empire in A.D. 70 and the dispersion of Judaism throughout the world is an example that could well be repeated by Tibetan Buddhism dispersed as it already is in India, Switzerland, France, Britain, the U.S.A. and elsewhere. Where Tibetan Buddhism persists in its traditional habitat and traditional forms it may assume a new significance. The growth in the number of 'Tibetan Buddhist' pilgrims (if that is how they may be described) coming from various foreign countries to Gangtok and Rumtek is perhaps a sign of this. Just as geo-political changes in the nineteenth century resulted in growth in new directions, so may changes of the same kind in the twentieth century. The growth of the strong Tibetan Buddhist presence in Darjeeling since 1960 may perhaps be seen, even if partly, as long-term compensation to Sikkim's Buddhists for what they lost when Darjeeling district was ceded to the East India Company in the 1830s.

At the time of writing a further turn of the wheel is bringing about a new policy of the Chinese government towards Buddhism and the recovery and rehabilitation of those Tibetan monasteries that have survived. It follows that Sikkimese Buddhist links with the north and with the *gumpas* of Tibet are likely to become important again, with consequences which must at present remain a matter of speculation.

Notes and References

1. Austine Waddell, (1894). *Lamaism in Sikkim,* (Reprint. New Delhi : Manjusri, 1978) , p.51.

2. Gerth & Mills. *From Max Weber*, p.293.
3. Gorer, (1938). *A Himalayan Village : The Lepchas of Sikkim*, (London : Thomas Nelson and Sons,) pp.215-252.
4. Gorer, *op.cit.*, p.189.
5. Gorer, *op.cit.*, p.193.
6. See the present writer's *Buddha's Philosophy of Man* (J.M.Dent: Everyman Library) 1983; pp.115-125.
7. See Waddell, *op.cit.*, (1894),pp.17f.
8. Hooker, J., (1855). *Himalayan Journals*, Vol.1 (New Delhi; Today and Tomorrow), p.132.
9. C.Von Furer Haimendorf, (1975). *Himalayan Traders* (London : John Murray), p.414.
10. With the exception of Nobling (or Nupling) where a *gumpa* was built in 1875, according to Waddell.
11. The demographic evidence in support of this view is as follows:

    In 1891, according to White's census taken that year (quoted by Waddell, 1894) the Bhutia/Lepcha population of Sikkim was 10,500. According to Waddell there were at that time a total of 985 lamas in Sikkim. This gives a ratio of lamas to general population of 1 to 10. In the 1931 Census of India the Bhutia/ Lepcha population was about 2.4 per cent. Making a projection on this rate of growth to the year 1944 a figure of approximately 27,000 for the total Bhutia/ Lepcha population is arrived at. In 1944, there were 1,071 lamas in Sikkim, according to Percy Brown's survey (Brown, 1944). It may thus be estimated that in 1944 the ratio of lamas to the Bhutia/Lepcha population had become 1 to 25. In other words, the percentage of lamas in the population had declined sharply during the fifty years from about 1894 onwards, from one in ten to one in twenty-five.
12. Trevor Ling, (1985). *Max Weber and Buddhism : The Rustication of an Urban Doctrine.*

CHAPTER 6

A Socio-Economic Study of the Pemayangtse Monastery of Sikkim

Ranju R. Dhamala*

Sikkim, a quasi-theocratic state till recently, had religio-political relations with Tibet from the middle of the seventeenth century. Buddhism came to Sikkim from Tibet as a proselytizing creed. The lamas, who came to Sikkim in search of sanctuary, took upon themselves the task not only of preaching their *Nyingmapa* (*rNying-ma-pa*) sect but also of setting up of a political order akin to its Tibetan counterpart. History records that after the three lamas of the *Nyingmapa* sect consecrated Phuntsog Namgyal as the first king of Sikkim, the Dalai Lama sent a congratulatory note bearing his seal, the mitre of Guru Rimpoche, the *Phurba* (dagger) and a most precious sand image of the Guru as presents. This gesture bound the new king to the Tibetan government and in times of crises, he looked to the Tibetan government for protection and aid.[1]

Among the three Tibetan lamas who visited Sikkim, Lhatsun Chenpo is remembered as the chief proponent of Buddhism in Sikkim. Besides constructing a number of monasteries and shrines he selected the sites for other monasteries. The oldest of them is at Dubdi, constructed

* Reader, Centre for Himalayan Studies, North Bengal University.

soon after the consecration of Phuntsog Namgyal. The monasteries of Tashiding, Rinchenpong, Sangacholling and Pemayangtse were constructed in the latter half of the seventeenth century or early eighteenth century. With the passage of time, the monasteries grew in size and number. At present there are 67 monasteries. In addition, there are 132 *Manilhakhang* (place of worship for ladies) and 22 *Lhakhang* and *Tsankhang* (hermitage or place of meditation).[2] Among these, six are considered the most important. Tashiding, Pemayangtse and Phensang monasteries belong to the *Nyingmapa* sect. These were either constructed by Lhatsun Chenpo or the sites were selected by him. The monasteries of Ralang, Rumtek and Phodong belong to the *Kargyudpa* (*ska-rbujud-pa*) sect. They were constructed during the time of the fourth Chogyal, Gyurmed Namgyal, in pursuance of a promise made to the Gyalwa Karmapa, the then Hierarch of *Karma-Kagyudpa* sect at the Tsorphu monastery in Tibet, during the former's visit there. These monasteries are endowed with vast areas of land and raiyats for their maintenance and they also enjoy tax exemption on these properties.

Location of monasteries

The site usually selected for a monastery is a commanding spot with a picturesque surroundings. The main building is a two-storeyed oblong structure. The lower storey houses the *lhakhang* or the prayer hall. The walls are decorated with frescoes depicting different gods and goddesses. For their services monks sit cross-legged on low seats facing one another in rows which stretching from the door to the altar. Nearest to the altar on a raised throne sits the Head Lama who conducts the ceremony. 108 lamps filled with butter burn continuously at the altar. The images of Buddha, Guru Rimpoche (*Padma Sambhava*) and Chenrezi (*Bodhisattva*) adorn the altar.

Purpose of the paper

Among the various monasteries of the *Nyingmapa* sect, Pemayangtse monastery (1706) occupies an important position. All the *Nyingmapa* monasteries in Sikkim are subordinated to it. Certain monasteries including Dubdi, Sangacholling, Linche and Pathing, and Ging in Darjeeling are directly under its control and they follow the rites and rituals according to the conventions of Pemayangtse. The head lamas of these monasteries are sent from Pemayangtse. The monks of Pemayangtse have the customary right of performing all the religious functions of the royalty. The head lama of the monastery alone has the power to consecrate the *Chogyal* of Sikkim. In spite of the high spiritual status accorded to these lamas, they were not unconcerned with the statecraft. Thus, they acted as royal advisers, fought in different wars against Nepal and Bhutan; represented the state in various treaties and negotiations besides fighting skirmishes at Rhenock, Namchi and other places against Nepalese immigrants. In the past this monastery enjoyed royal patronage both from Tibet and Sikkim.

The Pemayangtse monastery existed as a separate entity within the Sikkimese administration. Its religio-politico role cannot be underestimated. The changed socio-political situation of the state has certainly affected its earlier grandeur. The present paper attempts to study the impact of this change on the state of monastic affairs under two main headings : (i) personnel and (ii) economy of the monastery. I begin with a brief historical sketch.

History of Pemayangtse Monastery

Pemayangtse means perfect sublime lotus *i.e.* the monastery of perfect sublime lotus or *Padmasambhava*.[4] Regarding the construction and organization of this monastery two phases could be traced :

(i) Lhatsun Chenpo selected the site and constructed a shrine there. When Jigmed Pao, the third incarnation of Lhatsun Chenpo, visited Sikkim in 1709, he systematized the organization of monastic life. Besides initiating the Chogyal, Chagdor Namgyal and his son there to the mysteries of religion, he introduced a mode of chanting psalms and of performing ritual music, according to the system observed in the Mindoling monastery of Tibet. Jigmed Pao returned to Tibet after entrusting the management of the monastery to Kanchen Rolpai Dorjee.[5]

(ii) King Chagdor Namgyal along with Kanchen Rolpai Dorjee constructed the present building and laid down code of conduct for the monks. Pure Bhutia blood, good parentage, absence of any sort of physical blemishes were the chief qualifications for admission to the monkhood and celibacy was strictly enforced. No converts were admitted. King Chagdor Namgyal conferred an importance upon 108 monks and 108 families as their chief laymen. Its monks alone enjoy the status of *Ta-sang* (full monks of a monastic college). Although from its inception these monks enjoyed a privileged position, their position as the *Raj Gurus* in Sikkim was formally confirmed by the Maharajah Sidkeong Tulku as late as 1901. For the maintenance of its lamas and to meet the expense of religious performances, a vast tract of land was granted to it by the king Chagdor Namgyal. In 1901, Maharajah Sidkeong Tulku made a grant of certain legal rights in perpetuity. Thus the monastery enjoys not only economic control but also some judicial power over its tenants (*raiyats*).

Personnel

This section deals with the recruitment process, training, examination, promotion and hierarchy of the monastic order.

(a) *Recruitment and Training :*

It was the general custom among the people of Sikkim to send one son, normally the second, of the family to the monastery which is a reflection not only of the deep religious conviction of the people, but also of the social position and privileges accorded to the monks. In Pemayangtse admission is said to be stricter than at any other monastery in Sikkim. As we have seen above, admission is open only to children (boys only) of pure Bhutia blood, and they should not suffer from any sort of physical blemishes or deformity. They are admitted between the age of eight and ten. Before any formal admission is made, the parentage of the boy is thoroughly checked. If admitted, he is placed under the most suitable tutor after consulting the boys' horoscope. The final decision rests with the *Dorje-Lopon* and the *Umdze Lama*. Once the admission is confirmed the parents of the boy make an offer of food and beer to the monks and a great feast is held at the monastery to mark the boy's admission.

Under his tutor, the boy learns the preliminaries of writing and reading. He has to read and learn books of prayer and worship. During this period he stays with his tutor and renders menial service. This preliminary learning takes two to three years and it is then decided whether the boy can be admitted to the noviciate or not. If the boy turns out to be of low intelligence his dismissal is certain.

Entrance to the noviciate is of more significance than his first recruitment since it means that from now on the boy is subject to the discipline of the general monastic order. He is ceremoniously shaved, takes the vows of celibacy and poverty, assumes the dress of a monk and receives a religious name. These are, however, done only after a thorough examination of the boy's parentage, a physical examination, the giving of an entrance donation and an aptitude test by elder monks. The boy is asked to recite by heart the prayer he has learnt so far. The formal acceptance of the boy by the monastery is followed by presents from the novice's parents to the monks. These usually consist of a pig or a bullock, a load of rice and a load of beer according to their financial capacity. Once the boy is formally admitted to the monkhood, he is subjected to monastic discipline and rules and at the same time permitted to certain privileges of monkhood.

On the successful completion of period of probation, he becomes a junior monk. He is presented with a scarf of honour by the monks and is considered a member of their order. From that date he is relieved of the menial office of serving tea and beer to the monks and takes a higher seat in the Assembly Hall. A junior monk enjoys the status and privileges of fully ordained monks and is allowed to drink beer, hitherto untouched by him.

The second stage of training includes the art of making *torma* (votive offerings to the gods in the form of sacrificial cakes), blowing copper trumpets, playing cymbals, performing religious dances and the study of certain subjects, such as medicine, astrology and painting. It is found that most of the monks, if they choose at all to study any particular subject, take to painting. The monastery's frescoes and the *Zandog Palri* (copper-coloured mountain) depicting the heavenly abode of Guru Rimpoche as it appeared to Lhatsun Chenpo in a vision are testimonies to the artistic achievements of the monks. The *Zandog Palri* was made by Dungdzn Rimpoche single-handed in five years. It is an example not only of religious faith and perseverance but also of the finest skill in sculpture.

(b) *Examination :*

The first professional examination is held within a year of entrance to the noviciate, and in the following year or two a second examination is held to determine promotion. Until the novice passes these examinations, he has to serve tea and beer to the elders in the great Assembly Hall.

No written examination is held. The only procedure followed is to recite by heart all the prescribed books in the presence of the monks. On an appointed day all the elder monks assemble in the Assembly Hall, where the boy is brought by his tutor to perform the test, the first examination is conducted for three days, and nine intervals are allowed daily during the examination in order to enable the candidate to revise his exercises. The second examination, held after a year or two of the first, is conducted in the same manner.

The candidate is expelled from the monastic order if he fails at the examination for three consecutive years. However, if the boy is rich and seeks re-entry, the same can be done on payment of money and presents on a higher scale than formerly. If the rejected candidate is poor and he still wishes to continue religious life, he can do it only as a lay devotee doing drudgery about the monastery building or he may set himself up in some village as an unorthodox priest.[6] In short, only a complete recitation of various prescribed scriptures enables the candidates to pass the examination successfully. After these two professional examinations and admission to the monastic order, no further examination is held. Then they become junior monks.

(c) *Promotion :*

Once a novice is promoted to the position of a junior monk, his further promotion is determined according to the hierarchical pattern of the monastery. The promotion is automatic depending on the intellectual accomplishment of the monks and no examination is held for this. The hierarchical pattern (starting at the lower ranks) of this monastery is as follows :

(i) *Thungpo* or the conch-shell blower:

Two Junior monks are appointed to this post for a term of one year.

(ii) *Chapdip* or pourer of holy water :

This is also for one year.

(iii) *Konyer :*

He is the temple caretaker. He is in charge of dusting and arranging the altar, and making offerings of water, sacred food and removing the same from the altar. This post is tenable for three years. On the completion of these duties one passes the stage of *trapa* or learner and becomes an elder monk or *U-chho*. The *U-chho* alone can fill the higher posts of the monastery. They are :

(a) *Chinyer* :

Two monks are appointed to this post for three years. They are the store-keepers and in charge of the menials of the monastery. They are the link between the elder monks and the menial servants of the monastery. If the menials have any complaint it is communicated to the *Chinyer* who will inform the elder monks (*U-chho*) of this and place it before an assembly of *U-chho*. The decisions of this assembly is passed to the menials through these *Chinyers*.

(b) *Chotimpa* :

This is an important position which requires a person of deep learning, popularity, tact and ability to enforce discipline and respect. He is selected by a vote of monks and was approved by the king (presently, by the Ecclesiastical Department) for a period of three years. The *Chotimpa* is selected from one of the senior monks. He is in charge of the monastic library and one of his duties is to read out the monastic rules, maintain discipline among the monks and inflict punishment on the wrong-doers. He is required to lecture on religion and discipline occasionally to the assembled monks. He is the recognised head of the monks and their spokesman. He is usually reappointed for one or more terms.

The two offices of *Uchunpa* and *Kangsapa* do not fall in the hierarchical order althogh they are selected from among the *U-chho*. The *Uchunpa* is responsible for playing the cymbals and leading the service of the monastery in the absence of the *Umdza Lama*. The *Kangsapa* is responsible for the paraphernalia of worship in the monastery. His duties consist of lighting lamps, burning incense sticks, the preparation of prayer flags and so forth. These officials are selected from among the elder monks who do not have any specific duties and can be available to the monastery at all times.

In the last line of promotion are the two highest posts of *Dorje-Lopon* and *Umdze*. These offices are held for life and enjoy equal rank and privileges in the monastery. The division of function between them accords with the separation of spiritual and temporal domains. While the *Dorje-Lopon* upholds the dignity of religion by taking on part in secular matters and discharges his spiritual duties (which includes meditation), the secular matters of the monastery are looked after by *Umdze Lama*. He supervises the whole establishment and controls all discussion. It is to him that the villagers resort for advice and the settlement of disputes.

The economic administration of the monastery is looked after by *Thwimi* comprising five or six elder monks. The *Adda*-in-charge maintains the official record. The members of *Thwimi* are selected by an assembly of elder monks from amongst themselves. Those who do not hold any formal office in the monastic order are eligible. The final decision on their appointment lies with the *Umdze Lama*.

(c) *Monastic School :*

We can identify certain areas of change in the recruitment of monks particularly those caused by the establishment of a monastic school in 1960. The single teacher in this school is appointed by the Ecclesiastical Department in consultation with the elder monks of the monastery. Before the establishment of the school, new entrants used to be placed under individual monks after consulting the horoscope of the recruit, but now all recruits are admitted to the school and only one monk-teacher teaches them the preliminaries of reading and writing. The need for starting a school was felt because of the decreasing number of monks residing in the monastery itself. At present, although there is a total enrolment of 120 monks, only 40-50 stay permanently at the monastery. Most of them either have families to look after, or they work in government departments and schools and they assemble only during the principal ceremonies of the year.

Another important area which has consistently been affected by the modernization process is the economy of the monastery which is described below.

Economy

The Sikkimese monasteries possess large estates, the income from which is utilised for its maintenance and to meet the expense of religious ceremonies. The focus of this section is on the land management pattern of Pemayangtse.

(a) *General Pattern* :

There are six big monasteries in Sikkim.[7] 8 per cent of the total arable land of the state belongs to these estates. According to the Survey and Settlement Report (1968), the distribution of different categories of land in the monastery estates are as follows:

Table 1

Areas of arable land under monastery estate

	(in acres)
Panikhet (irrigated)	2696.78
Sukhabari (unirrigated)	15,213.80
Banjo (fallow/waste)	1830.35
Cardamom	2254.18
Orange groves (included in *Sukhabari*)	106.23
Total	22,101.34

(*Source* : "Survey & Settlement Report' (MS) 1?50-58, Government of Sikkim, Gangtok).

The monastery, instead of cultivating the land itself, leases it out to *bustiwallas* (secondary land-holders) who cultivate the land and pay taxes to the monastery. The number of such *bustiwallas* were as follows:

Table 2

Number of bustiwallas settled in monastery estate between 1950-58

Communities	*No. of bustiwallas*
Bhutia	2602
Lepcha	1432
Nepalese	4024
Total	8058

(*Source* : Survey & Settlement Report, 1950-58.)

The Bhutias held 914 holdings, Lepchas 909 and 884 holdings were with the Nepalis.

Regarding their management pattern, monastery estates can be grouped into two categories :

(i) monastery estates managed by the monastery wing of private estates (Rumtek and Phodong);

(ii) monastery estates managed by the *Udor-Tsosum* (managing body of the monastery)--(Pemayangtse, Ralang, Tashiding and Phensong).

(i) In the estates managed by the monastery wing of the private estates, the correction, transfer and mutation of the records of rights of land are solely in the hands of these private estates. The *Udor Tsosum* is not kept informed of the matter. The land rent, local rates and other taxes such as grazing fees, royalty from forest product, and cardamom *damthey khazana* are collected by it. Only a share of the revenue is given to the monastery for its maintenance and religious performances. The land rents are collected through block *mandals* who instead of getting commission for it receive tax exemption on their personal holdings.[8]

(ii) The estates of Ralang, Tashiding, Phensang and Pemayangtse are managed by the *Udor-Tsosum* (Managing committee) of the respective monasteries through their *adda*-in-charge. They are responsible for the maintenance of records and issue of revenue demands to the *bustiwal-*

las. Both land rents and local rates are collected through the block *mandals.* The revenue thus collected is utilised for the maintenance of the monastery and for religious performances.

The different categories of land in the monastery estates are (i) land directly held by the monastery as the primary holder, (ii) land leased out to the *bustiwallas* (iii) non-agricultural land.

(b) *Area of Pamayangtse Monastery Estate :*

The Pamayangtse monastery estate granted at the time of the king Chagdor Namgyal comprised a huge tract of land adjoining the monastery. In subsequent years, the size of the estate varied according to the political situation of the state. By a deed granted in 1730, the Phulbari land in the plains, then a Sikkimese territory, was given to the Pemayangtse monastery, including full rights on every plainsman *raiyat* who dwelt on the land.[9] Another deed granted in 1752 A.D. stated that Naxalbari in the plains were given to the *Avatar* of Dzongchen Lama and to Kanchan Rolpai Dorjee (both of Pemayangtse monastery) for their maintenance.[10] One notification issued by the Maharajah Sidkeong Tulku in 1901 mentioned that "according to the land settlement of 1888, the area of Pemayangtse monastery estate was confined within the four streams *viz.*, Rangit, Rathong, Khalet and Rimbi. However it could never take possession of the whole area due to some misunderstanding". It was during the time of the Maharajah Sidkeong Tulku that the area of Pemayangtse monastery estate was demarcated. Twelve blocks and two bazars were placed under it.[11] According to the land record of 1927-28, it had 14,391 holdings[12] out of which 1868 holdings were leased out to the *bustiwallas.* According to the State Administrative Report (1933-34), its total area was 19,091 acres with 435 households. In 1950-58, the area of total cultivated land and *khas* land under the Pemayangtse monastery was 9541.85 acres including the 90.15 acres of its home farm. In more recent times its area has come down to 6682.60 acres. It has 272.10 acres as its home farm. (*Survey and Settlement Operation,* 1982.)

(c) *Management and Income Pattern :*

The monastery has 12 blocks and 2 bazaars under it as its estate. The *Udor Tsosum* is responsible for the maintenance of records and issues *dhaddas* (revenue demands) for the collection of land rent and local rates from the bustiwallas. Both land rent and local rates are collected by them through their block *mandals*. Although landlordism was abolished in 1949 in the whole of Sikkim, the monastery was kept out of the purview of this legislation. Besides, the monastery enjoys the privilege of tax exemption. The whole of its revenue is to be utilised for its maintenance and for religious purposes.

The monastery estate can be classified into four groups: (i) land held by the monastery (primary holder), (ii) land leased out to people and registered in their names (bustiwallas), (iii) land held by household servants of the monastery (*chakareys*) and (iv) non-agricultural land held by the monastery (bazaar areas and the forest areas under its control).

Instead of maintaining the whole land under its direct control the monastery leased out lands to the *bustiwallas*, who had to pay the land rent at local rates to the monastery. In 1927-29, the monastery had 1868 holdings settled with 602 *bustiwallas*. The communitywise distribution of *bustiwallas* and the monks were as follows.

Bhutia	Lepcha	Nepali	Monks	Total
105	17	395*	85	602

Among the Nepalese Limbu tenants were numerous (136), followed by Chhetri (106) and Brahmin (50). 85 monks of the monastery owned 185 holdings. During the Survey and Settlement Operation (1982), it was found that out of 6682.60 acres of leased out land, 2489.44 acres belonged to the Bhutias, 237.82 acres belonged to the Lepchas and 3955.04 acres belonged to the Nepalese.

The status of *Chakareys* in the monastery estate is worth noting. *Chakareys* are the household servants of the monastery. They claim to have been appointed thus from time immemorial and is said to have carried on the work for generations. They are given lands free of rent in lieu of services rendered to the monastery and the monks. There are no written terms and conditions nor any job specification for these *Chakareys*. Generally every *Chakarey* family sends one member to the monastery every day or as and when required. Their tasks varied from cooking to carrying loads for the monks when they went for local visits or to Gangtok. It is the position of these *Chakareys* that had led the monastery into many legal suits. These will be discussed later.

Income of the monastery is derived from its agricultural output, its land rents and a subvention from the government.

According to the revenue record of 1927-29, the monastery had 186 plots (147 acres approx.) of land in its own name. Out of this there were 71 plots of dry field and 115 plots of paddy field. The total output from the dry products came to 127 *pathi* (1 *paṭhi* = 4 *seers* approx.) which included mainly maize, millet and buckwheat. From the paddy field the net output during this period was 490 *pathi* and 2 *manas* (8 *manas* = 1 *pathi*).

Out of the total 1868 holdings leased out to 602 *bustiwallas* during the same period, the total land rent came to Rs. 5127.11 *annas* (1 *anna* = 6 paise), Rs. 1796.00 was collected towards house tax, collected at the rate of the Rs. 2.6 *annas* per house. From its two bazaars, it collected house tax only. In 1927-29, is collected only Rs. 75/- from the Gyalshing bazar. The record of collection from Legship bazaar was not available.

In 1950-51, the collection of land rent including the fees on grazing field was Rs. 6,765.11. In 1973-74 Rs. 9,775.00 was collected towards land rent and other taxes.[13]

The budget estimates for 1975-78 were as follows :[14]

Table 3

Budget estimates for 1975-78

Year	*Anticipated Receipt (Excluding grain collection)*	*Anticipated expenditure*
	(in Rs)	(in Rs)
1975-76	22,730.04	13,030 + 81 md. of rice
1976-77	24,041.00	14,020 + 81 md. of rice
1977-78	28,481.00	15,674.50 + md. of rice

The total anticipated receipt for the year 1977-78 included :

1. Land rent and *dhuri khazana* (house tax)	:	Rs.	7,428
2. Cardamom *damthey khazana*	:	Rs.	6,251
3. Orange and Mango income	:	Rs.	1,500
4. Bazaar tax collection	:	Rs.	8,702
5. Forest royalty share	:	Rs.	4,000
6. Government Subsidy	:	Rs.	600
Total	:	Rs.	28,481

However in 1975, the Government decided to collect revenue of the monastery estates[15] through the District Collectorate and give a share of this collection to the monastery. Consequently, the monastery was debarred from collecting rents and rates from its estate, but at the same time the Government has failed to give a share of its revenue collection to the monastery resulting in its acute financial crisis. The monastery needs around Rs. 7062 annually for the performance of whole year's Puja, allowance to Kongsopa @ Rs. 30/- p.m. and to two *Konyer,* @ Rs. 14/- p.m. As a temporary measure the Government has been giving Rs. 2500/- to meet the expenses of daily service. Between 1978-80, the *Duchi* of the monastery was allowed to draw Rs. 7062 out of the monastery estate fund.

Changing Trends

Till the abolition of hereditary monarchy in Sikkim in 1975, royal patronage was crucial to the monastery's existence. However, the political changes in the state have also affected the monastery to some extent. To highlight the position of monastery under changed political situation, one case of land dispute between the monastery and its *Chakareys* is mentioned below.

During the rough survey of 1931-32, land holdings were recorded in the individual names of the *Chakareys* and consequently they were required to pay land rents and local rates. But in a joint petition, 26 *Chakareys* submitted that they would continue to render service to the monastery and enjoy land tax exemption but pay house tax which was at the rate of Rs. 2.6 annas per house. During the land survey of 1944-45, these lands were again recorded in the name of the *Chakareys*, but in response to a representation made by the monks of the monastery, the Land Revenue Department on 5th November, 1953 decided that the land of the *Chakareys* belonged to the monastery and the former were the secondary holders of monastery's land. They were required to pay only the house tax at the rate of Re.1/-.[16] Again during the survey operation of 1958, names of the *Chakareys* were recorded, but this time neither side raised any objection since the order issued by the Revenue Department in 1953 was being adhered to. Such a situation would have continued uninterrupted but for one incident *i.e.* the acquisition of *Chakareys'* land in the Kyongsa and Gyalshing blocks by the Agricultural Department. On acquiring the land the said department paid the compensation to the landlord *i.e.* the monastery and none to the *Chakareys* residing in the acquired areas. The *Chakareys* petitioned to the Government stating that the land acquired by the said department belonged to them and that the compensation should have been paid to them. Later the monastery agreed to pay 50 per cent of the compensation money to the *Chakareys*.

In July 1973, the Chief Secretary submitted a report to the Government stating that the compensation sanctioned in 1961-62 was equally shared with the secondary holders, in addition to the full compensation in respect of houses, fruit trees and stone fences, and if the secondary holders, wanted the compensation on the same principle as the primary holders, the Government was unable to comply with it, on the ground of agreement reached between the *Chakareys* and monastery lamas on 15th November, 1951.

Another Enquiry Committee was constituted on 26th July, 1973 to go into the grievances of these *Chakareys*. 'On the basis of various documents and Government notifications' the Committee concluded that the 1951 Royal Proclamation (order of Settlement Officer, Revenue Department) seemed 'to be little biased in favour of monastery authority' and recommended that the secondary holders of Gyalshing and Kyongsa be declared as primary holders and the other 50 per cent of the compensation be returned by the monastery and their rehabilitation to be considered by the Government. The Government approved the status of *Chakareys* as primary holders in August 1973[17] and the monastery refunded Rs. 50,962.52 only as compensation money to the villagers of Gyalshing and Kyongsa blocks.[18]

The monastery estate, which had hitherto enjoyed unquestioned privileges, came under the direct attack of the Land Reform Committee (1975), and beyond doubt, the land reform measures have affected the economy of the monastery.

In Sikkim, the idea of land reform was in the air since the late 40s. In response to popular demand, landlordism was abolished in this feudal state in 1949. Under the Government notification dated 20th August, 1949, it was decided that all land revenue previously paid to the agents of the estates would be directly paid to the government. By implication it meant the abolition of intermediaries. But fifteen estates which were part of the private estate of the Maharajah of Sikkim and five under the monasteries were exempted from this legislation. The Land Reform Committee (1975) for the first time expressed the need for the abolition of monastic estates.[10] It maintained that the existence of private estates and the monastery estate in political and administrative parlance could be seen as a separate organization operating largely outside the control of the Government. Control over agricultural and forest lands, the collection of land revenue, the maintenance of land records were held to be part of state activities in modern administration. Accordingly, it recommended the submission of land records hitherto held by the monasteries to the government for the correct assessment of land revenue and taxes. The homestead farm of the monastery along with the buildings and structure of the monastery were to be exempted from taxation provided they were recorded in the monastery's name. In regard to the imposition of a land ceiling it made three recommendations :

(i) exemption from the imposition of a land ceiling on the monastery's property,

(ii) restriction on the acquisition of additional land in the name of the monastery, and

(iii) abolition of the intermediary role of the estate with regard to the *bustiwallas*.

Of these three recommendations, the last one had a far reaching effect on the economy of the monastery as it meant that the monastery would cease to have the right to collect land rent and local rates from its *bustiwallas*. The taxes would instead be collected directly by the state, which would give a share of this revenue to the monastery.

Besides this, the Committee's main thrust of attack was on the status of *chakareys* of the monastery. It maintained "there are no terms and conditions laid down for this compulsory labour ... this practice seems to be most outmoded and this evil practice should be terminated forthwith".[20] It suggested that these *chakareys* should be given the same tenancy rights, status and so forth as are given to other tenants.

Although the implementation of the Land Reform Committee's recommendations ran into rough water, the State Government was prompt in withdrawing the right of the monastery to collect land revenue and local rates from its *bustiwallas.* At present the *bustiwallas* settled on the Pemayangtse monastery estate pay land rent and local rates to the State Government, the bazaar rates from its two bazaars (Gyalshing and Legship) are collected by the department of Local Self-government and the forest royalty is collected by the forest department. The Government is supposed to give a share of this revenue to the monastery but so far it has failed to decide the proportion to be handed over, thus depriving the monastery of its ancient sources of income.

An Overview

In Sikkim modernization looks like the import of an alien socio-economic and cultural regime. Since modernization has no native source, its impact on the cultural life of the area does not touch the core of it. This would appear to be substantiated by our study.

With regard to the privileges and position of the monastery two phases can be identified :

(i) The period upto 1973 when the monastery enjoyed royal patronage in terms of its religious, economic and judicial powers; and

(ii) the period after 1973, when democracy replaced the quasi-theocracy and the powers and positions of the monastery came into question.

At present, Pemayangtse, originally considered one of the most orthodox monasteries of Sikkim, is losing its former rigidity. In the recruitment, for instance, a degree of flexibility has crept in. The establishment of a monastic school has changed the pattern of the tutor-student relationship. Previously a monk had the right to use his pupil as his personal attendant, but now all the recruits are admitted to school under a single teacher, and this has changed the monastic routine too.

Pemayangtse was the only monastery in Sikkim where celibacy was strictly adhered to. The punishment for violating the vow of celibacy was expulsion from the monkhood, unless (i) it was his first offence, (ii) he prayed publicly for forgiveness, and (iii) paid a fine of Rs. 180/- and a second payment of his entrance fee and presents.[21] Equal importance was attached to the absence of physical deformity among all recruits. However, at present celibacy is not adhered to. The monks are permitted to marry including the *Dorje-Lopon*. In fact, the present *Dorje*-Lonpon is a married man and so the other monks. Absence of physical blemishes and deformity as conditions for the admission are not always followed.

As a result of land reform measures the monastery is deprived of a major source of income, and now depends on an annual grant of Rs. 2,500/- for its upkeep and maintenance, Rs. 600/- towards the expenditure of *Dhoop-Batti* given by the Ecclesiastical Department besides donations from its devotees. Moreover, more employment has been created in recent times and this has prompted monks to seek lucrative jobs in government offices and schools. Although the names of recruits enrolled in the monastic school number more than 200 at present it does not have more than 60 students. There are more than 120 ordained monks but the majority of them works outside the monastery and assemble only during the principal ceremonies of the year.

Denuded of its judicial, economic and political powers, the Pemayangtse monastery yet continues to serve the religious needs of the people. Even today it is a symbol of the deep religious faith of the Buddhists of Sikkim.

ACKNOWLEDGEMENTS

I acknowledge my thanks to Shri Ugen C.Lama, Lecturer, Centre for Himalayan Studies, North Bengal University for transliteration of Tibetan words.

Notes and References

1. Maharajah Thutob Namgyal and Maharani Yissey Dolma (1908). *History of Sikkim* (MS), para 94.
2. Government of Sikkim, *Sikkim District Census Handbook,* Gangtok, (1981.)
3. L.A.Waddell, (1959). *Buddhism in Tibet or Lamaism* (Cambridge : W. Hefferd & Sons,) p.258.
4. Some trace the etymology of the word to a vision that came to Lhatsun Chenpo. It is said that in his vision he saw a lotus in the lake situated on the top of the cliff. Later at the same spot he constructed a shrine after straining the lake. Hence the word *Pema* (lotus) *Yang* (cliff) *Tse* (top).
5. Maharajah T.Namgyal, *op. cit.*, para 120.
6. *Gazetteer of Sikkim* with an introduction by H.H.Risley, (Calcutta, 1874) p.330.
7. The Tashiding monastery estate was granted in 1949 after settling the areas adjoining the monastery with it.
8. *Mandals* are the revenue collectors. Previously they used to be appointed by the respective landlords.
9. Maharajah T.Namgyal and Maharani Yissey Dolma, *op.cit.*, para 165.
10. *Ibid.*, para, 196.
11. The twelve blocks under the monastery are Omchung, Kyongsa, Gyalshing, Chunbung, Topung, Darap, Nambu, Naku, Lurgzik, Singrangbung,. Sindaring and Singeng. Two marked under it are Gyalshing and Legship.
12. The average area of a holding is 8.06 acres.
13. Government of Sikkim, *Report of the Committee on Land Reform, 1975*. Deptt. of Land Revenue, p.26.
14. Based on the papers available at the Ecclesiastical Department, Government of Sikkim, Gangtok.
15. Vide Notification No. 1381/42, dated Gangtok, the 28th August, 1974.
16. In 1951 the rate of house tax was reduced to Re.1/- for the whole of Sikkim.
17. No. 579/LR(S) dated Gangtok the 22nd August, 1973.
18. Vide No. 580/LR(S) dated Gangtok the 22nd August, 1973.
19. Government of Sikkim, *Report of Committee on Land Reforms*, 1950-58, pp. 25-33.
20. *Ibid.*, pp. 27-32.
21. *Gazetteer of Sikkim* 1874, p. 302.

CHAPTER 7

Religion and Society in Tibet, Bhutan and Sikkim : a Bibliographical Study

Karubaki Datta*

Tibet, Bhutan and Sikkim, though situated in close proximity to India, present a pattern of religion and culture characterised by almost universal practice of *Mahayana* Buddhism. This religion has its own theory of government which unite spiritual power with secular and makes no distinction between the church and the state. The 'Dalai Lama', for instance, used to be both the religious and temporal head of Tibet.

Sikkim and Bhutan, while maintaining their national characteristics to a large extent, share the speciality of Tibetan culture through their common bond of religion. In addition, there are the Hindu Nepalese in Sikkim, Bhutan and Darjeeling and Christian converts from among the Nepalese and the Lepchas of Sikkim.

Its special characteristics notwithstanding, Tibetan Buddhism has received relatively little attention from the social scientists. Though there is no dearth of literature in general on the Buddhist states and the philosophical aspect of the religion, researches on religion in relation to society is not much in volume.

* Lecturer, Centre for Himalayan Studies, North Bengal University.

The purpose of this essay is to review the available literature on this region and to classify them broadly in accordance with their nature. The survey is based on published books and does not claim to be exhaustive.[1]

Tibet : Origin and Spread of Buddhism

Buddhism is said to have been introduced in Tibet in the seventh century A.D. Conversion *en masse* however took place later, in the eighth century, when Guru Padmasambhava visited the country in 747 A.D. and explained the philosophical, metaphysical and the mysterious elements of the faith that *Mahayana* Buddhism had developed in India after its breakaway from the *Theravada* school of thought. In the eleventh century, another Indian scholar, Atish visited Tibet and affected some doctrinal developments. Those included reforms in the religious life, abstinence *etc*. He founded the *Kagyupa* (*bka-brGyud-pa*) sect of religion, forerunner of the Gelugpa (*dGe-Lugs-Pa*) or the reformed church of Tibet. Buddhism in Tibet combined itself with the principles of another school of Buddhist thought, *viz*. *Vajrayana*. Its basic elements of faith were the *Tantric* practices, magical and supernatural powers obtained by religious practitioners through their initiation and meditative attainments. This incorporation was the result of the particular setting of Tibet.

In view of most of the scholars, prior to their initiation into Buddhism, the Tibetans practised Shamanism or the Bon religion. A second religion has however been identified by R.A.Stein. Different from Bonism, this was a 'churchless, doctrineless, priestless and almost nameless whole' best described as *Mi-chos, i.e.*, folklore or religion of man as distinct from *Cho-chos* or the religion of God, a term denoting Bon first and Buddhism later.[2]

In order to get assimilated to the Tibetan society Buddhism incorporated the services that these folk cults provided to the society. This in its turn strengthened the influence of *Vajrayana*. However all such elements overlapped and intermingled with each other in such a way that now it has become difficult to indicate the sources. The final shape that Buddhism has taken in Tibet is popularly known as Lamaism.

Once introduced to Tibet, this Buddhism generated a number of sects that shared all the basic elements of the doctrine but differed in their interpretations and emphasis on specific aspects of the rituals as well as the choice of some of the texts on which they concentrated their studies. The Buddhism professed by Guru Padmasambhava in Tibet came to be known as *Nyingmapa* (*rNying-mapa*) while Dromton, one of the followers of Atish became the formal head of the *Kadampa* (*bKa-gDams-pa*) sect, the forerunner of *Gelugpa* or the yellow hats. Two other sects that originated in the same century were *Kagyupa* and *Sakyapa* (*Sha-skyaka-pa*). Each in its turn was divided into sub-sects. Eventually, *Gelugpa* became the ruling order of Tibet.[3] The leader, with the help of the Mongols and the Manchus of China succeeded in proving himself the incarnation of *Avalokiteswara*. The Mongol ruler conferred on him the title 'Dalai Lama' or the Ocean of Wisdom.[4]

Literature on Tibet

Literature on Tibet is vast in volume and in time span ranging from the twelfth century to the present period. Particularly extensive is the literature on the philosophical aspect of Buddhism and its religious texts. Books on the history of Tibetan religion are many like the one by Helmut Hoffman (*Religion of Tibet*, 1961), that traces the history in its broad outline, compares Tibetan Buddhism with its Indian counterpart, describes the conflict with Bonism and the rise of the various lamaist sects.

A list of the books on Tibet has been made by A.Chand in his *Tibet : Past and Present : A Select Bibliography with Chronology of the Historical Events 1660-1981*. (1982)

Books describing the nature of Tibetan society and government can be divided into two groups : Travel accounts and Modern researches.

Travel accounts and personal experiences in Tibet

Difficult physical terrain and geographical isolation have, since an early stage, invited the curiosity of the foreigners. As early as twelfth century A.D. Marco Polo, the renowned traveller from Italy, had recorded detailed information about Tibet. His notes, based on hearsay are however not always reliable.

Many are the reports left by Christian missionaries at a later period. Most of such missionaries were attracted to Tibet by the possibility of founding a mission there and finding an ally in the person of Prestor John who, they believed, was a king of Tibet.

The possibility of a mission was brought to the notice of the Jesuits for the first time by a Portuguese merchant Diogo d' Almeida who reached Lhasa in 1600 A.D.. He mistook the Tibetans for Christians and his repõrts to this effect to the Archbishop of Goa aroused the curiosity of the Jesuit College there as a result of which Father Antonio de Andrade was sent to Tibet in 1624 A.D. Fr. Andrade, who left an account of his éxperience did not go into the heart of the country but stayed with the ruler of the province of Guge, bordering India. He returned to Tibet in the following year when he constructed the first Church of Tibet. He was followed by Stephen Cacella and John Cabral who travelled through Bhutan to Shigatse. Though welcomed by the ruler of the Tsang Dynasty they could not set up any permanent mission owing to the death of Cacella, in 1630 A.D.. Later, Tibet was visited by two more Jesuit priests, John Grueber and Albert de Orville, who travelled from China via Tibet and Nepal. Some original notes left by the Jesuits were summarised into English by C.Wessels in his book *Early Jesuit Travellers in Central Asia* (1924).

The Capuchins were more successful in laying their mission in Tibet on a strong foundation in 1707 that continued till 1745. The most important name in this context is that of Father Ippolito Desideri whose account of Tibet depicts the political and social conditions of Tibet at the time of Dzungar and Manchu invasions. An edition of this original account was published from London in 1937. Documents related to these missions, including a number of letters written by Desideri, either to his superior in Rome or to the Pope between the years 1713 A.D. and 1722 A.D. have been collected, translated into English and published by Fr. H.Hosten. They are compiled in the Volumes I, XXV and XXVII of his collected works. He has also collected some scattered documents related to the mission among which are the *Short History of the Capuchin Mission in Tibet by Rev. Fr. Felix of Antwerp OMC : Scattered Papers on the Capuchins of the Tibet Mission 1704-1720'* etc. *Tibet Hindustan Mission* by A.J.Osta (1959) also contain informations about the missions.

In more recent period, the Lazarist missionaries, Huc and Gabet, managed to reach Lhasa in disguise of lamas in 1846 after eight months' wanderings through Mongolia and China. Other missionaries were less fortunate in this respect. Miss Taylor had tried to enter Lhasa in the late nineteenth century but unsuccessfully. Experiences of these missionaries are recorded in *Travels in Tartary, Tibet and China During the years 1844-86* by Huc (1898) and *Travels and Adventure in Tibet* by W.Carey (first Indian edition in 1983) containing the account of the journey of Miss Taylor. The Norwegian missionary Theo Sorensen had undertaken several journies to Tibet in the early part of the twentieth century. These accounts are published together in the Volume 13 of the first series of the *Bibliotheca Himalayica* (1972).

Besides these missionaries, there were secular and religious scholars many of whom had tried to enter Tibet together a first hand knowledge of the country. The earliest of such accounts was left by George Bogle in 1774. He was followed by Turner in 1783. Both of them were sent from India by Warren Hastings on official mission, to review the possibilities of commercial relations with Tibet and to seek Tibet's assistance to solve India's border dispute with Bhutan. None of them was however allowed to enter Lhasa, the 'forbidden city'. Turner's narrative was published in a book form almost two decades after the journey itself, under the title *An Account of the Embassy to the Court of the Teshoo Lama in 1800.* Clement Markham in 1786 published with an introduction and notes the *Narratives of the Journey of Thomas Manning* -- the first Englishman to Lhasa. George Woodwork in his book *Tibet - the Early British Explorers* (1971) has discussed the travels of these Englishmen.

The official mission that followed Turner was that of Younghusband in 1903-04. The experience of that mission was published in 1905 by Perceval Landen who had personally taken part in it, under the title *Lhasa : the Mysterious City*. Simultaneously came out L.A. Waddell's *Lhasa and its Mysteries* (1905).

Throughout this period Tibet had been averse to the idea of disclosing her mysteries to the foreigners - Europeans and Asians alike. There were many private enterprises to cross the boundary, usually with the help of some of the Tibetan lamas themselves. John Macgregor's *Tibet : a Chronicle of Exploration* (1970) is a historical account of all these explorations, academic and adventurous alike. Similar in nature is *Expedition of Tibet : its History and Particulars* (1904) by Sandberg.

Experiences of such attempts have been written in forms of travelogues. They all describe the specialities of Tibetan society and culture in a narrative manner. Accounts like these include *The Land of the Lamas : Notes of the Journey through China, Mongolia and Tibet* by W.W.Rockhill (1891), *Diary of a Journey Across Tibet* (1894), by H.Bower, *Tibet : The Forbidden Land* (1898) by A.H.S. Landoor, *Journey to Lhasa and Central Tibet* (1902) by S.C.Das, *The Unveiling of Lhasa : High Adventure in Tibet* (1905) by E. Chandler, *Three Years in Tibet* (1909) by E. Kawaguchi, *To Lhasa in Disguise* (1924) by W.M.Macgovern, *Notes on a visit to Western Tibet* (1926) by H.Rutledge, *Secret Tibet* (1926) by F.Maraini, *Journey to Lhasa* (1927) by A.D.Neel, *Peaks and Lamas* (1939) by Marco Pallis, *In Search of Mahatmas* by E.G.S.Schary (date of publication not mentioned) *Tibet : The Country and its Inhabitants* (reprint - 1974) *etc*. Some more recent accounts include *Exploration in Tibet* (1950) by Swami Pranabananda, *Seven Years in Tibet* (1953) by Heinrich Harrer, *To Lhasa and Beyond : Diary of the Expedition to Tibet* (1956) by G.Tucci, *Tibet : Record of a Journey* (1957) by A.Winnington, *The Way of the White Clouds : a Buddhist Pilgrim in Tibet* (revised edition in 1968) by Lama Angarica Govinda *et al.*

Three narratives facilitate an understanding of the Tibetan setting because these were written out of an academic interest in Tibet and not a mere spirit of adventure. Waddell and S.C. Das were Buddhism scholars. S.C. Das published several articles on the history of Buddhism an some religious texts - published together in one volume in 1881 under the title *Contributions on the Religion, History etc. of Tibet* and another book, *Indian Pundits in the Lands of Snow* (1893). Waddell authored *Buddhism in Tibet or Lamaism* (1895). He also contributed an article on Buddhism to the Sikkim Gazetteer. A.D. Neel, scholar of Sanskrit language and literature, oriental philosophy and comparative religion, was the author of some books on Tibet, *viz. Initiation and Initiates in Tibet, With Mystics and Magicians in Tibet etc.* Rockhill worked on the religion, ethnology and geology of Tibet while Kawaguchi and Lama Govinda were Buddhist monks, Pranabananda a Hindu sannyasi, and Tucci a Tibetologist with several books on Tibet to his credit.

All of these writers were initially attracted to Tibet by the uniqueness of her religion and though some of them were prejudiced against and only superficially acquainted with the Tibetan culture and *Mahayana* Buddhism, most of them were primarily interested in the study of religion and highlighted its salient characteristics and organisational aspects. Even though they did not study the society from a social scientist's point of view, some of their observations do reveal a deep understanding of the Tibetan society and its attitude to life in general. Waddell, for example, observed that lamaism was not merely a monastic brotherhood but a truly popular religion deeply pervading and dominating the life of the people. 'It has given particular characteristics to the civilisation by setting before him higher aims, by giving milder meaning to its mythology, by discountenancing sacrifice and inculcating universal charity and tenderness to all living things. The tolerant spirit of Buddhism has stamped distinctly the national character, the mildness of which contrasts strongly with the rough exterior and the semi-barbarous state of people'.[5] G.Tucci observed in the national characteristics of the Tibetans in the twentieth century '(a) simultaneous sense of mystery and subjection at the same time', an attitude derived from the 'possession of the key opening the doors of mysterious or from the knowledge of the formula and rituals governing the play of comical forces. A quiet confidence that everything would conform to one's wishes, that human will triumph over the whims of malignant forces is a feature', that he felt 'had set Tibet apart from the rest of the world'. He also felt that the deep attachment of the Tibetans to the traditions and collective sub-conscious had obstructed the development of human personality and individualism of the accident that leaves room for the initiative of the individuals to strike out for himself, with the lonely soul as its only guide'.[6]

Tibetan life appeared typically medieval, comparable to the societies of medieval France and Burgandy to Fosco Maraini, yet the Tibetans seemed to him to be a 'really happy people -- so far as people can be happy on this earth'. This happiness he analysed not in terms of social structure or form of government but as 'a question of equilibrium between the world by which he is surrounded and the world he carries in his heart'.[7]

Such observations are in total contrast to the characterisation of the Tibetan society by the pro-Chinese authors like Han Suyin (*Lhasa : The Open City : A Journey to Tibet,* 1977) and Israel Epstein (*Tibet Transformed,* 1983). Written with the aim to justify the Chinese takeover of Tibet, they describe religion of independent Tibet as nothing but means of oppression, especially for the women that encouraged corruption, immorality, homosexuality *etc*. Chinese takeover of Tibet, the Chinese sources say, has not only freed Tibetans from the clutches of religion but also opened up avenues for industrialisation and material uplift. This gradual transformation was noted by Epstein during his three extensive tours in Tibet, the autonomous region of China in the years 1955, 1965, 1976. Time that had been 'made to stop in traditional Tibet had started to move under the Chinese rule' and, 'they had been freed from the total theocracy' that had resulted in the 'most terrifying exploitation and impoverishment' and 'kept them in total ignorance and terrorised them into total submission' -- commented Han Suyin.[8]

Though these remarks are biased by the tendency to justify the Chinese action and therefore not to be accepted as they are, there is no doubt that the Tibetan society has indeed changed materially after the Chinese occupation. Winnington in his *Record of a Journey* (1957) has described the economic changes that were setting in in Tibet at that time. This has been admitted by Thubten Figme Norbu (*Tibet*, 1969), who otherwise describes the Chinese takeover as a mere disaster.

Modern Researches

Mahayana Buddhism, as it developed in Tibet, was closely linked to the governmental politics and so deep was this relationship that it became totally integrated with political, social and even economic institutions of the country. Religious teachers in Tibet provided not only spiritual but also political leadership. The uniqueness of Tibetan government has been observed and pointed out by all the visitors to the country but not much research has been done to analyse the nature of this government and politics. Franz Michael's *Rule by Incarnation : Tibetan Buddhism and its Role in Society and State* (1982) is a pioneering work in this respect. The functions of the state were divided into religious and secular, but, both were closely linked and no line of demarcation could be drawn between the two. The Dalai Lama was the head of both. This system, despite its external appearance of a 'theocracy' was not a theocracy in the strict sense of the term because Buddhism does not recognise any 'Theos' or Supreme Being, but rather a spiritual essence in which all the beings partake. The degree of enlightenment reached by each being in its present existence determines its future existence in a chain of rebirth, the final goal being the break of this chain of rebirth and physical existence and attainment of *Nirvana*, a state of undefined bliss. Yet this commitment to religious ethics does not rule out the scope for internal modernisation and does conform to the modern concept of state. This is the basic thesis of Michael, which sharply contrasts to the characterisation of the Tibetan government by Tsung Lien Shen and Shen Chi Liu (*Tibet and the Tibetans,* 1952). By analysing the nature of Tibetan society in terms of division between subjects and masters they do not even attempt to measure the administration by a 'modern yardstick' as that would be a 'waste of time'.[9]

Michael goes on to show that in spite of status distinctions in the traditional society it always had room for social mobility by providing channels to higher status and higher education through provision for admission to monastic life. This ever open access to higher status siphoned off chances of peasant rebellions or demands for agrarian reforms. Access to higher income was also guaranteed through encouragement of commercial business, practice of crafts and accumulation of private property -- which, being exempted from tax, in its turn formed the financial prop of the urban middle class. When faced with crisis, in the early decades of the present century, the Tibetan government also proved responsive to the needs of modernisation of army and introduction of western education. These attempts failed due to some reasons but the government succeeded in proving its compatibility with modern needs of the society. The adaptability is well reflected in the adjustment that the Tibetan refugees have made in the changed circmstances in India. This has also generated the feeling of nationalism, a characteristic of modern state. This analysis, in some respects, bears similarity to the characterisation of the Tibetan society by the Dalai Lama, the ruler himself (*My Land and my People,* 1962). Pointing out the scope of social mobility guaranteed by the monastic organisations ensuring higher education and status even to a low born as also to the unsuccessful beginning in the direction of change of the social system from 'medieval' to 'modern', the Dalai Lama explains that it is wrong to presume that Buddhist doctrine of *Karma* and rebirth discourage a man from trying to improve his lot.

In this context, mention should be made of Bina Roy Burman's book, *Religion and Politics in Tibet* (1979). In this she has examined, quoting secondary sources, the religious conditions in Tibet since 1959 when China finally annexed Tibet, introduced changes and imposed curbs on religious activities. Han Suyin and Israel Epstein in their books, already mentioned above, have pointed out the changing attitude of the Tibetans towards religion as well as the inroads that the revolutionary ideas of Marxism - Leninism have made into the Tibetan society.

A Cultural History of Tibet (1968) by David and Hugh Richardson and *The Tibetan Civilisation* (1972) by R.A. Stein contain sections on the nature of Tibetan society and government. According to Stein, Tibet is an 'ecclesiastical' state rather than a theocratic one with regard to both the central government at Lhasa and the more or less independent local states. Almost all the Tibetans, from the bottom of the social scale imbibed a deep and sincere faith and this, according to them, gives them the very characteristics of medieval man. Then, in order to explain this, the author describes the political and economic aspects of organised religion that plays a no less extensive role in the country's intellectual life.

Bhutan : initiation into Buddhism

It is widely accepted by the scholars that Bhutan received Buddhism from Tibet. Even though tradition has it that Guru Padmasambhava had personally visited both Bhutan and Sikkim during his travels in Tibet in the eighth century A.D. it is suggested on the basis of historical evidence that the conversion of Bhutan to Buddhism had taken place in the fifteenth century. Fifteenth century Tibet witnessed a serious ideological conflict and struggle for supremacy between the *Gelugpa* and the *Karmapa* (*bK-rMapa*) sects as a result of which, the *Drukpas (aBrug-pa)*, a sub-sect of *Karmapa* was forced to find a new home in Bhutan. They converted the country into Buddhism. B.C.Olschak's *Ancient Bhutan : A study on Early Bhuddhism in the Himalayas* (1979) is a history of the phases of such religious propagation with documentary evidence from some ancient Tibetan texts.

The view that Bhutan received Buddhism from Tibet has however been contradicted by B.R.Chakravorty in Volume I of his *Cultural History of Bhutan* (1979). On the evidence of archaeological ruins in Suryapahar in Assam and elsewhere, he argues that Bhutan, being closer to Buddhist seats of learning at Vikramsila and Nalanda than to Tibet received her first lessons of Buddhism from India. Cattle herders, traders, travellers and mendicants came in contact with Buddhism in the plains of Assam and Bengal and carried it to Bhutan. As in Tibet, Buddhism underwent change in Bhutan too, under the strong influence of Bonism, the indigenous religion of pre-Buddhist period. This theory, original in itself, awaits further evidence before it can be proved conclusively.

Literature on Bhutan

Bhutan has received lesser attention from the travellers and scholars than Tibet. It is mentioned only in a few travel accounts like that of W.A. Waddell (*Among the Himalayas*, 1899). The nature of the travel accounts in general has been discussed in the previous section.

Apart from these narratives, the literature on Bhutan can be put under two broad categories : I. official reports and II. modern researches.

Official Reports

The awareness about this neighbouring state of India originated in the last quarter of the eighteenth century when dispute broke out between Bhutan and the state of Coochbehar over the question of boundary. Official missions were despatched to Bhutan to induce better relationship between the two countries and to seek Tibet's assistance to solve the problem. The first mission was that of Bogle in 1774-5, followed by that of Turner in 1783, K.K.Bose in 1815, Pemberton in 1837, Eden in 1863, Rennie in 1865 *etc*. To this body of literature may be added the narrative of J.C.White, the political officer of British India for Sikkim and Bhutan (*Sikkim and Bhutan : Twentyone Years on the North East Frontier*, 1909).

The reports describe in particular the form of Bhutanese government with the two authorities of Deb and Dharma Rajas, the religious institutions and the socio-economic organisations. These accounts differ in their attitudes towards the Bhutanese people and society, descriptions varying according to the treatment they received at the Bhutanese court as well as the achievements of the missions. Bogle and Turner were impressed by the people and their social manners as with the warmth and sympathy in the court. They spoke highly of the people, praised their simplicity of manners, strong sense of religion and trustworthiness. K.K.Bose, who does not otherwise probe into the religious practices of the people, testifies to a pervading sense of religion among the common people. J.C.White's remarkable narration also is characterised by a sympathetic and understanding attitude towards the people. His description of the lifestyle and nature of the Bhutanese and the Sikkimese people are regarded as authentic in some respects till today. Some reports of the nineteenth century, on the other hand are less favourable towards the

Bhutanese. Pemberton and Eden, for example, had become disappointed with the failure of the mission and their bitterness found expression in the accounts of, among other things, the religious practices and monastic life in Bhutan. The lamas, in Eden's view, were nothing but 'idle, good for nothing and illiterate set of men, ignorant as a rule, of the tenets of religion they profess to teach'. They are also accused of being the 'most sensual and immoral specimens' of the 'most immoral race of the world'.[10]

Modern Researches

Recent studies on Bhutan, including those by Ram Rahul (*Modern Bhutan,* 1971), L.E.Rose (*The Politics of Bhutan,* 1978), and Nari Rustamji (*Bhutan : The Dragon Kingdom in Crisis,* 1978) are many in number. Their discussion mainly centres around the question of political relations with India, political developments in modern times and general description of life in all its aspects. Since religion and politics were intertwined in Bhutan, they touch upon the socio-religious specialities of the kingdom. Yet few probe thoroughly into the nature of interdependence between religion and state. From this point of view, literature on religion and society of Bhutan is negligible.

Bhutan, like Tibet, had a special form of government till 1907. It made no distinction between the church and the state and theoretically at least all power was concentrated in the church. In practice, it was a 'dual' system, the actual running of affairs being divided into sacred and secular authorities, between Dharma and Debrajas. This system, as it developed in Bhutan, failed to define the functional relationship between the two authorities. This 'dual' system, at the time of its birth had implied a total subservience of the state to the religion. All the lay officials had to assume a semi-monastic character before high positions and the nature of the state could be best described as 'semi monastic'. In practice however, it created elements of conflicts, specially during the infancy of the Dharma raja and the retirement of the Deb rajas.

Michael Aris, in his book *Bhutan : The Early History of a Himalayan Kingdom,* (1980) has analysed the contradictions in the nature of the state in short. The basic theme of the book is reconstruction of the ancient history of Bhutan from written Tibetan, archaeological as well as oral sources as expressed in the myths and legends. Besides containing historic facts, they reveal the psychological attitudes of the society for which the legends and myths act as a statement of truth.

Sikkim : a Religious Profile

Buddhism was introduced in Sikkim at a comparatively later period of seventeenth century. Following a feud in Tibet among the various religious sects and subsects, a group of *Nyingmapa* lamas fled to Sikkim. There they installed Phuntsog Namgyal as the king in 1642. Thus started the process of conversion of the Sikkimese Lepchas into Buddhism. At present there are only two schools of Buddhism *Nyingmapa* and *Kagyudpa* in Sikkim. The *Nyingmapa* represents the unreformed style of Buddhism tinged with Bon religion. They rarely practice the Buddhist principles of celibacy and abstinence. It is interesting to note that despite the existence of only two sects in Sikkim, monasteries belonging to the *Kagyudpa* sect are only three in number in Rumtek, Ralang, Phodong. The remaining monasteries being to the *Nyingmapa* sect. Buddhism ceased to be the state religion in 1975 when it was proclaimed a part of the secular state of India.

The religious and ethnological profile of Sikkim is complicated by the existence of the Lepchas -- believed to be the original inhabitants of the country and the Bhotias belonging to the Tibeto-Burman stock. Buddhism in Sikkim, while retaining the basic principles of *Mahayana* Buddhism, has assumed a different characteristic distinct from that of Tibet by its amalgamation with the Bon religion practised by the Lepchas in the pre-Buddhist period.

During the nineteenth century, the picture was further complicated by the Nepalese immigration and the simultaneous introduction of Hinduism, professed by the majority of them. Christianity has also managed to convert a group of Lepchas and the Nepalese.

Literature on Sikkim

Sikkim, like Bhutan, has received lesser attention from the travellers and scholars. Travelogues, exclusively of Sikkim are wanting though travel in Sikkim has been described by those explorers, who, on their way to Tibet had passed through Sikkim. A bibliography has been compiled by S.C.Schappert, under the title *Sikkim : 1800-1968* (occasional paper

No.10 of the East West Centre Library of Honolulu, 1968). Apart from the titles of the books on Sikkim it includes list of official and governmental documents related to Sikkim.

Travel accounts containing information on Sikkim include the already mentioned narratives by Ronaldshay, Kawaguchi, A.D.Neel and Sir Richard Temple's *Travels in Nepal and Sikkim* (1887) as well as *Himalayan Honeymoon* (1940) which is a description of a journey to Lachen and Zemu Chu by way of Phalut and contains brief notes on Sikkim. The Appendix III of *Indian Pundits in the Lands of Snow* by S.C.Das (1893) contains a narrative by Nabin Chandra Das -- *A Trip to Sikkim* which is an excerpt from the diary of his journey in 1877 to South Sikkim. Nor are there many official reports barring those by J.C.White J.W.Edgar (*Report on a Visit to Sikkim and the Tibetan Frontier in October, November and December*, 1873) and Macaulay (*Report on a Mission to Sikkim and the Tibetan Frontier*, 1884). Reference to Sikkim is scattered in D.F.Rennie's *Bhootan and the Story of Dooar War* (1866). J.D.Hooker's *Himalayan Journal : Notes of a Naturalist* (1855) deserves a special mention in this context. Though a botanical scientist, Hooker, in his account gives occasional description of life and society of the people of the regions he visited. *The Gazetteer of Sikkim* edited by Risley (1899) containing articles by J.C.White, L.A.Waddell is till today the most widely used handbook on Sikkim. In the chapter on religion, Waddell pointed out the special characteristics that *Mahayana* Buddhism developed in Sikkim and explained the ritualistic rites, monastic hierarchy *etc.* at great length.

Modern Researches

Modern researches on Sikkim on the theme of relation between religion and society are not many in number. Recently A.C.Sinha has written a book on the political history of Sikkim where he has discussed the political institutions in the context of ethnographic, religious and social patterns (*Politics of Sikkim*, 1975). Most other studies concentrate on the description of history of Sikkim and its annexation by India.

One segment of the Sikkimese society -- the one composed by the Lepchas -- has received considerable attention from the anthropologists.

Besides the articles by Captain Campbell, C.Jest, K.K.Das, Rene von Nebesky Wojkwitz, there are books by J.Morris (*Living with the*

Lepchas : A Book about the Sikkim Himalayas, 1938), H.Siiger (*The Lepchas : Culture and Religion of the Himalayan People*, Parts I and II, 1967) and G. Gorer (*Lepchas of Sikkim*, originally published under the title *Himalayan Village : An Account of the Lepchas of Sikkim*, 1938). A recent publication of particular interest is *Lepcha : My Vanishing Tribe* by A.R.Foning (1987).

A particular feature of the Lepcha religion is the simultaneous practice of the two apparently contradictory religions of Munism and Buddhism. In spite of some basic differences between the two, there are some external resemblances like the ambivalent nature of the supernatural beings, the predominance of the priests, interpretations of dreams, beliefs in horoscopes, *etc*. The Lepchas have sterilised and ignored those aspects of Buddhism that opposed their major existing attitudes and accepted only those that resembled their own religion. Buddhism therefore accommodated the principles of Munism and assumed a particular form among the Lepchas. This is admitted by Foning, a Lepcha himself. Gorer explained the reason of this as a lack of any formal training in the scriptures of Buddhism on the part of the Lepchas. The Lepchas, due to a lack of knowledge of alphabet, were not able to read the scripture by themselves at the time of their conversion to Buddhism. Nor were they admitted to lamaseries for formal training and instructions. Thus, their conversion did not mean much to them. Foning further points out that even the Lepcha translations of the Buddhist scriptures, when done, were not done literally, care being taken to see that the books suited the people for whom they were intended. Even the translation of the biography of Guru Padmasambhava was with a true Lepcha air, he argues. Lama Lhatsung Nankha Jigma, who introduced Buddhism to the Lepchas made contacts with the native priests and learned from them all the inherent beliefs of the Lepchas which he later incorporated into the already existing Buddhist creed. Foning mentions the rituals and the worships which were thus accepted. He admits that the Lepchas understand very little or none of the actual Buddhist rituals and modes of worship. Though they can identify themselves with some scriptures which have been translated into their language, they fail to understand the more important sections of the Buddhist doctrine of incarnation, the idea of previous births, the damnation of sin in the after life, *etc*. Their superficial understanding of Buddhism and absence of any institutional control on them have resulted into their recent conversion to Christianity which seems to have left a deeper impact on their character than what Buddhism had been able to do. Christian converts exhibit a strong sense of sin which otherwise is absent from the Lepcha ethics in general. Indira Awasti in her book, *Between Sikkim and Bhutan : The Lepchas and Bhutiyas of Pedong* (1978) has tried to explain the reasons of Lepchas' conversion to Christianity. In addition to the absence of guidance, financial consideration also played its role. Being economically poor, they embraced Christianity readily because it freed them from the observations of costly rituals like those of death.

Conclusion

On the basis of the above survey it is possible to highlight some characteristics of the literature.

The main thrust so far was on Tibet. Interest in Tibetology originated in the eighteenth century 'Orientalism' when the western scholars developed an interest in the history and culture of the East. East itself was influenced by this and an interest in its own cultural heritage was born anew. This interest in Tibetology was confined mainly to the study of Buddhism that assumed a particular form in Tibet and also to a little extent in Bhutan and Sikkim. There are not many works in the other religious groups, their interaction with the impact upon each other. Even in modern times, when the social perspectives have undergone a change due to economic developments and greater interaction with the outside world, social science researches on the role of religion in Sikkim and Bhutan are lacking in number.

However, some new trends have set in during the past few years. Scholars are trying to use modern research methodologies and interdisciplinary approaches to study these overwhelmingly 'theocratic societies' of the Buddhist states as well as the 'primitive' tribes like the Lepchas of Sikkim. These modern works, though few in number, are more analytical and qualitatively different from either the descriptions of the official reports prone to prejudiced outlook and superficial understanding of the societies or travel accounts and academic papers by Tibetologists dealing with religion in its philosophical or ritualistic aspects.

Notes and References

1. English translations of books in other languages are also mentioned. Attempt has been made to give, as far as possible, the original date of publication. In case of reprints and revised editions, in English or in any other language, the publication date of the later edition has been given only when the original date is not mentioned in the book.
2. R.A. Stein, (1972) *Tibetan Civilisation* (London: Faber and Faber), pp. 164-5, 191-99.
3. Almost all the books on Tibet give the history of the different phases and characteristics of Tibetan Buddhism in short. For details see L.A. Weddell -- *Buddhism in Tibet or Lamaism* (Cambridge: W. Heffer & Sons Ltd., 1959) and G. Tucci -- *The Religions of Tibet,* (English translation, Bombay: Allied Publishers, 1980).
4. F. Michael, (1982). *Rule by Incarnation : Tibetan Buddhism and its Role in Society and State* (Boulder: Westview Press), p. 40.
5. L.A. Waddell, *op.cit.,* pp. 566-573.
6. G. Tucci, (1956). *To Lhasa and Beyond* (Roma; Institute Polygrafico dello Stato), pp. 95-101.
7. F. Maraini, (1954) *Secret Tibet,* English translation, pp.147-148.
8. Han Suyin, (1977). *Lhasa, The Open City : A Journey to Tibet,* (New York : G.P. Putnam's Sons), p. 19.
9. Tsung Lien Shen and Shen Chi Liu, (1952). *Tibet and the Tibetans* (Stanford : Univ. Press), p. 112.
10. A. Eden, (1972). *Political Missions to Bhutan Bibliotheca Himalayica,* Series I, Vol. 7 (New Delhi; Manjusri Publs. House), p. 126.

CHAPTER 8

The Inter-active Pattern of Hinduism and Buddhism in Nepal

Gopal Singh Nepali*

Nepal has certain contextual features which render the functioning of society somewhat different from that of India. First, it is the marginal land of caste -- the meeting-ground for the people of caste-society with the people of non-caste society of Tibetan affiliations. Secondly, it is the land where, unlike in the plains of India, the tribal groups do not constitute an island in the sea of caste but meet their Hindu counterparts on terms of equality; thirdly, it is the place where Hinduism, Buddhism and local 'animism' have been inter-acting upon each other and making their respective demands on the local people in consequence of which each of these religions has resorted to syncretic process and modified themselves to suit the local requirements of life and finally, caste is the basic structural principle for the organization of society not only for the Hindus but also for the Buddhists. The concept of purity-pollution cuts across religious lines and even the Tibeto-acculturated tribal ethnic groups are brought within the purview of this conceptual framework in handling social relations.

Broadly the people of the hills can be divided into three groups—the Nepalese speaking *Parbates*, who are orthodox Hindus; the Newars who

---

* Professor, Department of Sociology and Anthropology, Tribhuvan University, Kathmandu, Nepal.

mostly live in the Valley of Nepal and are divided into Hindus and Buddhists; and the Tibeto-Burman tribal groups who occupy different points on the socio-cultural ladder of the Nepalese society. These groups constitute, respectively 58.4 percent, 3.0 percent and 9.1 percent in the total population of Nepal. In contrast, they constituted 48.7 percent, 4.7 percent and 17.2 percent in 1951. Thus it would be seen that the Nepalese speaking group is fast increasing its population, while the proportion of the Newars is declining sharply with its untold consequences for the survival of Buddhism in Nepal. For, Buddhism is the religion of these Tibeto-Burman groups and of a section of the Newars. According to 1981 Census, the Buddhists accounted for 5.3 per cent of the total populations, while the Hindus accounted for the 89.5 per cent in contrast to 7.5 per cent and 89.4 per cent in 1971 respectively. Such a proportion in 1952 - 54 was 8.6 per cent and 88.9 per cent. Thus it again clearly indicates a downward tendency in the proportion of the Buddhists.

But despite the declining proportion of the Buddhists as compared to the politically and numerically dominant Hindus, Buddhist cultural life is the dominant theme in the Valley of Kathmandu with its monuments, shrines, arts and crafts, religious beliefs and practices, feasts and festivals.

Both Buddhism and Hinduism seem to have a remote antiquity in the history of the Valley. In the different periods of its known and unknown history, hordes of Hindus and Buddhists from the plains of India are reported to have gone into the Valley of Kathmandu where they met the Mongoloid people from the north. The Valley with its fertile soil as drained by the Bagmati rivers and its tributaries and with its salubrious climate provided the most ideal place for the meeting of such migrants from India and from the north. It had functioned as an important market centre for the exchange of goods between the traders from India on the one hand and Tibet and China on the other. And for centuries it functioned as a crucible for the melting of the different cultures and races, and out of it arose a complex culture which the world knows as the Newar culture in which Buddhism took on a variety of a new kind.

The people who developed this culture is known as the Newars, the speakers of Newari, a Tibeto-Burman speech. In the whole of the southern Himalayas, it is only the Newar and the Ahom who have a script and literature of their own among the Tibeto-Burman languages. The

Newars were responsible for the creation of a high level of culture in the Valley with their excellence in architecture, metal and wood-work. One section was Buddhist (*Buddhamargi*) and the other Hindu (*Sivamargi*). They carried on a tradition of maintaining a harmonious relation between the two major universal religions. The testimony to this is borne by the abundance of existing Hindu and Buddhist shrines, rituals and festivals in the valley of Kathmandu.

These Newars are divided into endogamous castes and sub-castes whether they are Hindus or Buddhists. They are further split into numerous secular occupational groups, each having a patron-deity of its own to preside over its respective occupation. Caste cuts across religious boundaries. The following is the Newar caste hierarchy in a descending order :

Table 1

Newar Caste Hierarchy

Hindu Castes			*Buddhist Castes*
I. High Castes	:	*Deo Brahmin* *Chatharia Shrestha* *Panchtharia Shrestha*	*Bajracharya* *Bare* *Udas* (metal worker)
II. Peasant Castes	:	*Jyapoo* or *Maharjan*	
III. Unclean Castes *(Ekthari a)*	:	(1) *Manandhar*, (2) *Gathu* (Gardener), (3) *Nau* (Barber), (4) *Khoosa* (Vegetable grower) (5) *Chitrakar* (painter) and (6) *Chheepa* (Clothdyer)	
IV. Untouchable Castes	:	*Duniya-Balami-Sanga* *Bha* (who accepts death-gifts) *Kasai* (Butcher) *Kusle* (Priest to low castes & receiver of death-gifts) *Pore* (basket-maker and public executor) *Chyam-Khala* (Scavenger caste) *Kullu* (Newar Cobbler) *Hara-Huru* (lowest type of Scavenger).	

Of these, the high castes include the *Bajracharya, Bare, Udas* and *Gyapoo* peasants (of Kathmandu and Patan area) who are all Buddhists.

On the Hindu side the high castes include *Deo Brahman*, the *Shrestha* and *Gyapoo*. A number of households among the *Chhatharia Shresthas* of Kathmandu still calls themselves Buddhist. All the *Ektharia* castes (called single bodied castes) are Buddhist and employ a *Bajracharya* as family -- priest. Among the low castes such as *Bha, Kasai, Kusle*, Buddhism is the officially accepted religion, though members of their castes are the *Deopalas* (temple caretakers) at the Hindu temples of Ganesh, Bhairava and Bhairavi.

But caste cuts across religion and there is no bar to marriage if caste is the same.

The co-existence of Hinduism and Buddhism in the Valley of Kathmandu is the outcome of such social organization of the Newars based on caste hierarchy. Both the religions had existed side by side right since very remote period of history of the valley. The antiquity of the shrines of Swayambhu Nath (a Buddhist god treated as primordial Buddha) and Pasupati Nath (Lord Siva) points to the early introduction of both of these religions in the Valley. Besides, the Hindu and Buddhist legends both claim the existence of Hinduism and Buddhism right from the time when the Valley was believed to be a lake.

However, authentic evidence of the existence of Hinduism and Buddhism could be checked with epigraphic records not for the period earlier than the middle of the fourth century or the beginning of the fifth century. The epigraphic records, rich as they are, suggest that towards the middle of the fifth century, Buddhism and Hinduism were existing side by side. A reference is found to king Vrasadeva, who ruled sometimes in the later part of the fourth century or the beginning of the fifth century. He is said to have been a Buddhist and to have built several Buddhist monuments including the famous *Chatya* of Swayambhu Nath. These epigraphic records also suggest that Buddhism in the Valley were supported by the people, who were socially, ethnically and linguistically diverse. Though Buddhism was never dominant in the society of those days, it grew and prospered under the royal patronage and its shrines were honoured equally with those of Hinduism and Vaishnavism.

Yuan Chwang, a Chinese pilgrim of the seventh century A.D. informed in India that there were some 2000 monks of both the *Hinayana* and *Mahayana* kind in the Nepal Valley. But what exists today in a representative form is the *Vajrayana* Buddhism without monastic institutions.[1] It appears that the early monastic institutions (*Vihara*) got abolished due to reasons unknown and these places became the abodes of the married clergymen, the *Bajracharyas*, who act as family-priest to the higher caste Buddhist Newars, enjoying an analogous status to that of a Brahmin priest. The old memories of monastic ascetism are now preserved by the three initiation rites to be undergone by the male children of the *Bajracharyas, viz., Barechhuigu, Achaluigu* and *Dekha*. These rites are intended on the one hand for symbolic entering into monkhood, and on the other, qualifying and initiates to achieve the status of a *Bajracharya* to perform their religious role as family priests.

As stated earlier Newar Buddhism is of the *Vajrayana* variety and without monks. And without state patronage, even though a minority religion, it has wonderfully survived and co-existed with Hinduism in an interactive role. Rather than dying out, it has, through syncretic processes, incorporated many Hindu divinities, cults, ceremonies and festivals to rejuvenate, itself while at the same time allowing Nepalese Hinduism to absorb many of its elements. The close identity between these two religions could be possible because of incorporation into each of them the local animistic cults which provide explanation to the local conditions of life in terms of rain, agricultural prosperity, diseases and sickness and the need for triumph over the forces of nature. Such animistic gods and goddesses abound in the Valley and are richly reflected in Hinduism and Buddhism of Nepal.

The interdependence between Hinduism and Buddhism can also be seen through the mutual attitudes between these religions as found in their respective sacred literature. Thus the Nepal *Mahatma* teaches through the mouth of Parvati that to worship Buddha is to worship Siva. The Buddha is explained by the Hindus as an *avatara* of Vishnu. As the tenth *avatara* of Vishnu, Buddha had to come to preach against the horror of the Vedic sacrifices recommended by the Vedas. There is a particular day marked when the Buddhist *tiara* is placed on the phallus of Pasupati Nath. As the Nepalese legends go, Naga Takshaka (a serpent god) is associated with Buddhist gods, and Garuda with Lord Vishnu. When there was a conflict between the two, Lord Vishnu took side of Garuda, and so Buddha had to come to the rescue of his servant - Takshaka. Ultimately the conflict ended in friendship, and Takshaka coiled himself around Garuda's neck as a token of friendship. Consistent with such traditional explanation, an idol of Garuda with a snake around its neck is worshipped by both the religious sections of the Newars in the Vallev even today.

There are many shrines in Kathmandu where the same idol is worshipped as a Buddhist god by the Buddhists and as a Hindu god by the Hindus. Thus God Mahakal at Tundikhal is worshipped by the Buddhists as their most important deity Padmapani, a Bodhisattwa. On the other hand, the Hindus worship it as a form of Bhairava. The images of god Manjusri at the temple of Mahakal and at Swayambhu is a male god for the Buddhist whereas the Hindus worship it as Saraswati.

Another set of deities common to the Buddhist as well as the Hindu Newars are the *Ajima*. They are seven in number and are believed to preside over the various kind of poxes. These malignant deities have got to be propitiated very frequently. In every domestic ceremony of the Newars, *Ajimas* are represented symbolically and worshipped along with other deities to insure that no untoward things happen in the family.

Two other important deities occupying a prominent position in Newar domestic ceremonies are Bhairava[2] and Ganesh. At home, Bhairava is represented by a jug of rice-beer and Ganesh by a betel nut placed on a heap of rice. Outside home, every locality has a temple each of Ganesh and Bhairava. Another variety of deity which characterises the socio-religious life of the Newars is the 'Chhwasa' -- a place marked at the nearest crossing of the roads. Chwassa is believed to be the dwelling place of a malignant spirit. It has to be propitiated daily and also at the time of all domestic ceremonies by offering it food in a leaf cup. Both the Buddhist and Hindu Newars invariably follow this cult.

Another deity which is commonly believed in and worshipped by the Buddhist and Hindu Newars is *Nasa-Deya*. It is a dancing Siva whose image is engraved on the back-walls of the temples. This deity presides over dance and music. As each Newar caste has a musical group for providing music for their socio-religious purposes, the cult of *Nasa-Deya* cuts across religious and caste lines.

Of the gods commonly accepted by both the religions include : Manjusri (As Saraswati among Hindus), the eight mothers, Brahma, Vishnu, Siva, Ganesh, Bhairava, Agni, Bhagwati (generally known as *mai*), Kali, Narain, Matsyendra-Nath, Kumari (Virgin Goddess), Bhimsen, Laxmi, rivers, mountain-tops, nagas (Serpents), tanks and pools. How they are worshipped in their particular form and style will be clear in the sequel.

If one analyses the deities and cults of the Newars, one finds that both of them have absorbed some common elements of 'animism' which are characteristic of the autochthones of India, particularly the Mundas. It seems that there was a time when the people of the Austro-Asiatic speech lived in all over the Himalayan region and provided substratum to the culture of those who migrated to these regions. This is not only suggested by the Mundic linguistic features to be found in the Tibeto-Burman languages of the Southern Himalayas, but also by the cultural practices of these people. Thus the cult of earth-deities so dominant among the Newars along with the cult of Bhairava[3] as well as many festivals in which a mock fight takes place between the followers of Indra (The leader of the Aryans) and of the followers of Bhairava do provide some suggestions of the legacy left behind by the earliest settlers of India.

Another source from which common elements could be incorporated into Hinduism and Buddhism of the Valley was the Natha ascetics who played an important role in the formation of the religious beliefs and practices of Nepal. The cults of Matsyendra Nath, and Gorakh Nath with the local legends woven around them indicate this. The Kusles among the Newars who accept death-gifts on the seventh day claim to be the former *Natha* ascetics who became degraded subsequently. They are at present considered a low caste and follow tailoring as their secular occupation. Besides, they provide ritual music in the Newar worships. They also act as *deopalas* (care-taker) at the Ganesh and Bhagwati temples.

Vaishnavism seems to have played an important role in matters of the religious formation in the Valley. The Valley has four prominent temples in honour of Narayan, one of which called Budanilkantha is linked to the king of Nepal. The king is believed to be the incarnation of this god. This belief is common both to the Buddhists and the Hindus. The *Jyapoos* (peasant Newar caste) have particular association with the cult of Narayan -- no matter whether they are Hindus or Buddhists. Many among them have Narayan as their lineage god. Besides, there is an annual festival in which the Jyapoos keep on display at each and every street the pictures of Krishna at the time of the festival called 'Krishna

Jatra'. The numerous idols of Narayan that have been dug up the earth indicate the strength of the cult of Narayan. Its association with the Newars seems to be deep and unavoidable. For, it is invariably associated with the organization of marriage and family among the Newars. The ceremony of Yihi is a great event among them. When the Newar girls attain the age of 5 to 6, they have to be married with an emblem of Narayan with the bel-fruit as the witness. It is the sacramental marriage of a Newar girl. After that a Newar woman is free to divorce, in theory, her human husband and remarry as many times as she wants, since her real husband - God Narayan - is immortal. This is equally practised by the Buddhist and Hindu Newars.

The cult of female worship, probably due to the influence of *tantric* beliefs, is equally shared by the Buddhist and the Hindus. This cult is represented by the numerous temples of Bhagwati, worshipped as Kali, some as Buddhist Yogini and some as simply Bhagwati. The lowest form of this deity is to be found at the cremation grounds where she presides over the burning of the dead and is represented by rounded stones. These are temples whose care-takers (*deopala*) belong to the untouchable castes. They also preside over the various kinds of diseases, particularly, measles and small-pox. These are the deities who are dreaded and have therefore to be propitiated. Both the Buddhist and Hindu Newars worship at the temples of these deities with an equal degree of fear and concern.

What is typical of the Newar religion is the worship of the goddess Bhagwati in a human form, called Kumari. Every locality has its locality-Kumari; every town has its town Kumari; and then there is Kumari at the National level. A girl from among the Buddhist priestly caste -- *Bajracharya* - is selected to become a Kumari after making her to undergo a series of tantric rituals. She is removed and replaced by a new one when she reaches the age of puberty. At every important ritual event, whether of domestic nature or of community nature, the human Kumari has to be worshipped. The Buddhist as well as Hindu Newars worship her without fail.

The Kumaris who head the three towns of Kathmandu, Patan and Bhatgaon have political functions also. Even the present Gorkha king of Nepal has to play a role in relation to the State Kumari of Kathmandu who owns a palace opposite to the ancient palace of the Newar kings. She has a *Bajracharya* priest to perform her *'nityapuja'* (daily worship) and a retinue of attendants.

Continuing in the tradition of the Newar kings, the Gorkha king of Nepal performs certain rituals in relation to goddess Kumari. He has to visit her temple (her palace) and worship her. The human goddess puts a *teeka* on his forehead and offers a sword to him. This symbolises a mandate from the human goddess Kumari to the king to rule over the Valley of Kathmandu for another one year. Thus again it symbolises interdependence between the two religions.

The festival held in honour of Kumari is a Buddhist festival. The human goddess Kumari is placed on a chariot which is dragged through a fixed route in the city of Kathmandu. She becomes the object of veneration and worship by all the inhabitants of the city. Her chariot is accompanied by another chariot in which a boy representing Ganesh is installed. At the wheels of these chariots there are images of Bhairava, which are given bloody sacrifice before starting the procession. Thus the complex of Kumari, Ganesh and Bhairava reveals the Newar religious skill of effecting a compromise and cooperation between Hinduism and Buddhism.

Another deity of political significance is the Talleju Bhawani -- the family deity of the Malla kings. Her huge temple stands on a high pedestal within the precinct of the Newar palace. She is a tantric goddess believed to have been brought into the Valley by Nanya Deva, a Karnataka Chieftain who established the Karnataka dynasty in the Valley around the tenth century A.D. She is a deity worshipped by the Buddhist and the Hindu Newars equally. She is offered annual buffalo sacrifices on behalf of state for nine days during the *Nava-ratri*. The Gorkhali king has to worship her on a particular day. This goddess epitomises the glories of the Newar kings, and is the object of special veneration by the Newars. The Parbates also worship her but only as a form of Bhagwati. Such a different emotional orientation of the Parbates and of the Newars becomes discernible on the eighth of the *Navaratri*. While the Parbates on this day are assembled at the historic Kotquadri-angle to worship and offer animal sacrifices to Gorkhali flags and weapons, the Newars throng to the temple of Talleju Bhawani, the deity representative of their cultural greatness.

The temple of Guheswari at the bank of the river Bagmati is a Buddhist tantric goddess. She is culturally associated with the Newars though the *Parbate* Hindus worship her as one of the *pithas*. It is believed that when Siva roamed about in the different parts of the country with the dead Parbati on his shoulder, the different parts of her body fell at different places. The vaginal part fell at Kamrup, while the anus part fell at Kathmandu. Thus the place where the anus of Parbati fell became the abode of the goddess Guheshwari. It is to be noted that the care-taker (*deopala*) of this temple is a *Kasai* which is an untouchable caste among the Buddhist Newars, while *Nitya Puja* is done by a Buddhist priest. She is worshipped both by the Buddhist and Hindus, the former believing her to be a *tara* and the latter a form of Parbati.

The festival of Bhairava Jatra on the 1st of the dark half of Baisakh is purely a Buddhist festival. This is known as *Indra-dwajosthanam.* A huge wooden pole is erected in which the Buddhist priest officiates and the members of the *Manandhar* caste (oil-presser) associate themselves right from the time of bringing the sal-tree pole from the forest to erecting it at Newar king's palace. At the time of the erection of the pole, the Parbate king is represented by a sword and a contingent of the Brahmin State-priest (*Rajguru*) in their traditional military attire present a march-past and salute the pole. This festival marks the advent of the new year of *Vikram* era. A similar festival is held in the town of Bhatgaon. There too the Buddhist caste of *Manandhar* is ritually associated with the festival.

The greatest of the festivals of the Newars known as Matsyendra Jatra is held in honour of a Buddhist god Matsyendra Nath who is identified with *Avalokiteshwar* or *Padmapani.* This god epitomises the agricultural prosperity in the Valley. The role of this god is to ensure that no Newar goes hungry. It is also regarded as a rain-god and the Newars -- especially their peasant section -- invest the name of this god with deep emotions and call it *Karunamaya* (the one who is full of piety) or Bungadeya. K.P. Chattopadhyaya believes that this god is an amalgamation of three different cults, *viz.*, the cult of Bungadeya (the rain-god of the pastoral people of the Valley who lived in the forgotten past), Saint Matsyendra Nath --- the teacher of Gorakhnath and the Avalokiteshwara or Padmapani Bodhisattwa. The Chariot dragging the idol of this god starts from his ancient temple at the bank of the river Bagmati towards the southern extremity of Patan and lasts for one month. It finally ends at the parade ground at Patan town with the display of the shirt of this god. It is a great national event and all the Newars go to worship at the Chariot. Throughout the period of the *Jatra*, the images of Bhairavas engraved on the wheels and the front of the Chariot are offered goat sacrifice. They eat ritual food called *Samaya* after the Puja. The chariot of Matsyendra is accompanied by the Chariot of Ganesh; the elephant-headed Hindu god who is equally believed and worshipped by the Newar. This entire festival is manned by the Newar Buddhists, the *Bajracharya* priests, who are in this official role called *Dharmis*.

Such instances of common deities, cults and beliefs followed by the Newars under two official heads of Hinduism and Buddhism can be multiplied without number. What is noteworthy is that Buddhism and Hinduism have a thin dividing line in Nepal. One is Buddhist or Hindu because one employs a Buddhist priest (*Bajracharya*) or a Hindu priest (*Deo-Brahmin*) in addition to claiming himself as a follower of the Buddha or Siva. Thus it seems that Buddhism has managed to exist in Nepal for exactly the same reasons for which it declined and ultimately disappeared from India. In India, Buddhism could not survive after the withdrawal of the Royal Patronage whereas in Nepal, even when the powerful minority in the form of a ruling class not extending patronage to it, it managed to survive because of the popular support it based itself on. This is what Michael Allen thinks. This seems to be a possible explanation even on the basis of the data analysed in the preceding pages. Every religion has to adapt itself to provide certain functions, besides enabling its followers to attain spiritual goals. In the case of Newar Buddhism it had to face a twofold problem. First, the royal patronage was no longer available to it especially when orthodox Hindu rulers were patronising Hinduism. Secondly, Buddhism had to provide mundane functions to its adherents as Hinduism had been doing. By accepting the caste system, the institution of family priest-hood parallel to that of the Brahmin priest and many of the functional gods which explained local conditions of life, Buddhism offered practically all that which Hinduism was giving to the people. Hence, the popular base of Buddhism became a reality. There was no need for being a permanent monk for attaining ultimate salvation. In other words, Buddhism in Nepal got modified itself to the service of its adherents for fulfilling their numerous mundane needs as a matter of practical adjustment. Such a process of modification is also found among the neo-Buddhists. By becoming Buddhists they have neither abandoned caste nor their traditional culture which made their life meaningful.[4]

Notes and References

1. The opening of a series of *Hinayana* monasteries in the Valley is a recent innovation which has no relation to Newar Society.
2. The Buddhist priestly caste *Bajracharya* venerates it but rarely goes to worship at its temple.
3. It is believed that there are 8½ lakhs Bhairavas and a great number of serpent gods (*Nagas*) in the Valley.
4. Gopal Singh Nepali, (1965). *The Newars : An Ethno-Sociological Study of a Himalayan Community* (Bombay : United Asia).

CHAPTER 9

The First Phase of Roman Catholic Presence in the District of Darjeeling (1846-1900)

G. Kottuppallil*

Introduction

Since the middle ages, legendary tales about the inaccessible lands of India, Tibet, and China were popular in Western Europe. Rare, vivid, romantic accounts by daring travellers like Marco Polo fired the imagination of both the adventurer and the missionary to explore these mysterious lands in search of wealth and Christian allies,[1] that these lands were reported to hold in abundance.

The discovery of India by Vasco da Gama while shattering on the one hand, the myth of 'a powerful Christian country' that India was supposed to be, increased on the other hand, the western curiosity about the hidden land of Cathay which they believed Tibet to be. It was a common opinion that a large Christian community had fled from India to Tibet at the time of the Muslim invasion. Several missionary expeditions were organized and sent to explore this unknown land since the later middle ages.[2]

* Librarian, Sacred Heart College, Shillong.

Countries like Nepal, Sikkim and Bhutan were important to the Catholic missionary in as much as they offered safe routes to Tibet.

The first Christian missionaries to enter the eastern Himalayas were the Jesuits Stephen Cacella and John Cabral in February 1627. They were cordially welcomed at Cambirasi but made to stay on there for over six months. They utilized this time to learn Tibetan for the purpose of translating the 'catechism' and prayers into Tibetan. Finally they reached Shigatse, a royal city of the eastern kingdom of Utsang.

Fr. Cabral had to return to Hoogli (Bengal), the Portuguese headquarters for provisions and personnel. Since Cacella was uncertain about Cabral's fate, he too left for Hoogli after a year long waiting. At his arrival at Hoogli, Cabral had already left for Shigatse with another companion, Fr. Manoel Dias. Fr. Cacella too, though in weak health, hastened to join them. Unfortunately Manoel Dias fell ill at Morung in the Terai and died on 3rd November, 1929 -- first in a long list of Europeans whom the Malarial fevers of the *Terai* was to claim. Cacella died at Shigatse on 6th March, 1630 and was given a solemn burial befitting a lama. Cabral was soon called back by his superiors to work in south India.[3]

In 1704, Rome appointed the Italian Capuchin missionaries to evangelize Tibet. They remained at Lhasa from 1707 in a vain attempt to establish Christianity in Tibet, till they were compelled to abandon the Himalayan country and betake themselves to Nepal in 1745. The conquest of Nepal by the Gorkha king Prithisinarayan Shah ended their hopes of Christianizing even this country which had appeared initially susceptible to Christianity.[4]

Darjeeling under Patna Vicariate (1846-87)

It was R.J.Loughnan, ICS Judge of Patna, who convinced Archbishop Carew, Vicar Apostolic of Bengal of the suitability of the newly opened Sanatorium of Darjeeling for the sick European missionaries. The Archbishop conceived the idea that such a place would soon be popular with parents who wanted a suitable place in India for the schooling of their children. In 1846, he sent four sisters of Loreto to Darjeeling with Mother Teresa Mons as superior along with a chaplain, Fr. McGirr, to establish a school and a rest house for the missionaries.[5]

At the establishment of the Vicariate of Patna in 1845 Sikkim had been put under its ecclesiastical jurisdiction. Hence when Mgr. Anastasius Hartmann, the Swiss Capuchin bishop of Patna, discovered that Carew had already founded an institute at Darjeeling which was originally a part of Sikkim, he successfully claimed his jurisdiction over the district and while Carew recalled his priest, a Capuchin took his place as the chaplain to the sisters and to the handful of Catholic soldiers.[6]

The Loreto School

The decision to go ahead with the girls' school was a bold one since to begin with there were as many teachers as pupils. In 1847 the number of pupils increased from 6 to 17 and the year after to 24. During the first 17 years the number seldom went up beyond 50.[7] Then the numbers started picking up every year. From 1880s, when Darjeeling was connected by railway, the convent school was in great demand with the European and Anglo-Indian population from the plains of Bengal and Bihar.

The attention of the Loreto sisters was not limited solely to the European and Anglo-Indian children. From 1855 they had small section of the school set apart for the local boys and girls. From 1868 till 1887 they conducted also an orphanage which was then transferred to Loreto Entally (Calcutta). One of these local children later joined the sisters as Sr. Josephine Bridget and brought into the church her whole family. Adult baptisms became a normal feature of the convert. However no separate institution was built solely for native apostolate, till 1903.[8]

The Capuchin chaplain, Fr. Ignatius Persico,[9] with the encouragement of Mgr. Hartmann started St. Gregory's school for boys. Two years later, Persico was transferred to Bombay as Hartmann's secretary and with it the school too was closed.

In 1877 Mgr. Tosi, then Vicar Apostolic of Patna started again a school for boys in Darjeeling. Since the Society of the Holy Spirit Fathers who had been working till then in Chandernagar refused the offer of the school, the Capuchins themselves couducted it at "Sunny Bank", under the name of "St. Joseph's Seminary".

A few Seminarians from Patna joined the school which totalled 34 students in 1881. The institute offered courses till B.A. However, the

Catholics of Calcutta preferred the famous Jesuit educationists to run the institute at Darjeeling and repeatedly petitioned the Holy See to this effect. Finally in 1887, the Holy See handed over the whole district to the Archdiocese of Calcutta and the Jesuits bought the St. Joseph's Seminary from the Capuchins and after a few years transferred it to the present site of North Point. Under them St. Joseph's College became the most important educational institute of the district totalling by 1895 over 200 students.

A dispute over Darjeeling

As for other Europeans, for many a healthy missionary, Bengal had proved to be their tomb due to its excessive humidity, heat and malarial environment. Hence, since the days of Archbishop Carew they pleaded with Rome for some territory in the cooler hills of the Himalayas. The Apostolic Visitor Mgr. Charbouneaux had recommended in 1861 that the vicariate of West Bengal be given Darjeeling and the prefecture of Central Bengal the town of Hazaribagh.[10] However Capuchins held on to Darjeeling and ceded instead Hazaribagh to the Jesuits of Calcutta. But Hazaribagh was unsuitable as a health resort and Rome was again requested by the Jesuits of Calcutta and the Milanese missionaries of Krishnanagar for hill towns in Darjeeling district. Rome succeeded in making a compromise between the two groups of missionaries in 1881 ceding Kurseong and the Terai to the Jesuits of Calcutta and Sonada to the prefecture of Central Bengal (Krishnanagar) while the Capuchins held on to Darjeeling after wrestling from the Jesuits a promise not to open any educational institution in their area. In 1887, however, the Apostolic delegate Mgr. Ajati persuaded the Capuchins to relinquish their hold over the rest of Darjeeling in favour of the Jesuits who could conduct schools in the hill town better than the former.[11]

This dispute over the district put off by three decades any serious apostolic work in the district. The Capuchins were few in number and could not spare more than one missionary for the entire district. The Jesuits would have been instead in a position to care for the district as they had at their disposal, more men and resources.

DARJEELING UNDER THE DIOCESE OF CALCUTTA

The Jesuits in Darjeeling

Fr. Accursio, OFM Cap., had baptized a number of Nepali families in the course of his long stay at Darjeeling. The Jesuits Fr. Weinandy and

Fr. Fiereus developed this community which increased from 30 in 1887 to 90 in 1890.[12]

Under the care of Fr. Alphonse Schaelaecken, the Catholic community witnessed further growth and development. In 1893, a new school was built for the benefit of the local children to whom he gave much attention. But the disastrous cyclone of 25th September, 1899, which wreaked havoc upon the entire district through the numerous landslides it caused, destroyed the school. The teacher and his family who lived there, lost their lives.[13] In 1893, Fr. Schaelaecken also built in the vicinity of Loreto a more spacious and beautiful church for the growing Catholic community.

In 1902, Fr. Louis Bodson took over the ministry among the Lepchas and Nepalis of Darjeeling. The school for girls that he built to be looked after by the Loreto Sisters, had a short life, as we saw above. But his school for boys attracted pupils of all castes and creeds and developed into a popular institution.

Fr. Ford, who worked at St. Joseph's North Point, developed another small Christian community of about 50 persons around the college complex, as many of them worked there. In 1898, a chapel was built for them there. That community too saw a steady growth ever since.

Catholics in Kurseong

The arrival of the Jesuit seminarians in January 1889 to this little town boosted its importance. While seminarians and staff busied themselves with their philosophical and theological studies, they also found time to cater to the needs of the local population.

It was Bro. Didier with his medicines who made St. Mary's College Kurseong a popular health centre for the sick people of the little town and neighbouring villages. Initially he used to visit the sick in their homes but as the crowds at the dispensary increased he sent a lay catechist on that mission. In 1895 a new dispensary was built near the College.

Fr. Motet, a zealous missionary among the tribes of Chota Nagpur, on his arrival at Kurseong as Professor, took up also the charge of the local Catholics. In 1890, a school and orphanage, named after St. John

Berchmans was established. Two years later the Christian community got their first church. In 1895, the first girls' school was established. The 'Daughters of the Cross' took over the direction of this school and that of St. Margaret's orphanage in 1899.[14]

The 'Daughters of the Cross' who came to Kurseong in 1890 completed the spacious "St. Helen's Technical School" in 1900 and attracted many girls from near and far. Training in culinary, tailoring, nursing, stenography, book binding, music, painting, *etc.* was imparted to the students. In the decades following the school too increased in the number of its students.

Work in other regions

The Jesuit missionaries were eager to move out of Darjeeling and Kurseong to evangelize the Lepchas and Nepalese of the villages. However their attempts were thwarted each time by the uncanny opposition of the protestants exercised through the government authorities. In 1900 Fr. A Schaerlaecken tried to found a mission Centre and school at Linding but did not succeed in his attempt. Bodson who established there a school was forced by the authorities to stop it. His efforts to start another school at Takdah was also likewise halted by the Government. The Scottish mission's monopoly over the establishment and running of schools for local children had telling effect on their adversaries -- the Roman Catholics !

The professors from St. Mary's college, Kurseong ministered to the growing tea-garden population of both the Terai and Dooars. The Dooars was under the ecclesiastical jurisdiction of the Bishop Krishnanagar who requested the Jesuits to cater to the tea garden workers. As the missionaries were mostly veterans from Chotanagpore, they knew Oraons, Mundas and Kharias and their culture and ministered to their spiritual and material needs. The tea-garden planters were of great assistance to them in constructing schools and chapels for the children of their workers.

Work of the Foreign Missionaries of Paris (MEP)

The Holy See had appointed the foreign Missionaries of Paris to the Tibetan missions. China who claimed suzerainty over Tibet was most unwilling to permit any European mission -- arise into Tibet. The French

Lazarist missionaries from Mongolia, Joseph Gabet and Everista Huc, had visited Lhasa and surveyed the possibilities of entering Tibet through Assam. The MEP men lost no time to request Rome for Assam and obtained it as part of Tibetan mission. But their efforts to enter the forbidden land ended tragically when their missionaries, Nicholas Michael Krich and Augustine Bourry, were killed by Kaisha, a Mishmi chieftain, in 1854 in the land of the Abors.[15]

In 1856, missionaries Auguste Desgodius[16] and Louis Bernard attempted to traverse through Sikkim and then Nepal but the rulers of both the countries formally refused their requests. So too their efforts to reach Tibet through Ladakh, though successful, was short lived. Hence the MEP men were recalled and sent to China from where later they entered the Chinese occupied areas of Tibet. But even from their every effort to reach Lhasa was thwarted. In 1880, A. Desgodins was once again sent by his bishop from Eastern Tibet to enter Lhasa from the South. Arriving at Calcutta on 5th September, 1880 he prepared himself for his mission by securing the permission of the Viceroy himself to enter Sikkim. In April 1881 Desgodins and Henry Mussot made Darjeeling their temporary home while surveying the land east of the Tista for a possible centre and printing little books in Tibetan on Christian doctrine. In November 1882 they were given the permission by the District Commissioner of Darjeeling to settle at Pedong. The Lt. Governor of Bengal approved of the decision on 19th Jan. 1883. Rome assigned the ecclesiastical jurisdiction over that territory to them to establish a centre for later expeditions to Lhasa. By August 1884 they built a two storeyed house while converting their temporary dwelling into a school.

This subdivision, east of the Tista comprised about 2000 families at that period. About 800 of them were Nepalese, 600 Bhutanese, and the rest Lepchas or Limbus. The initial aim of the missionaries was to Christianize as many Bhutanese as possible as they were Tibetan in culture in order to build a Tibetan Catholic community. However only a handful of Bhutanese entered the Roman Catholic fold while the Nepalese and Lepchas were more open to the Christian religion.

On 2nd November, 1890 a well instructed group of Nepalese were baptised. In 1891, the government leased out a large forest area to the mission destined for its Catholics. Fr. John Marie Hervagault who had come in 1883 to substitute Fr. Mussot moved over to this area and founded the Christian village of Maria Basti near Pedong. A chapel and 12 little houses formed the nucleus of this village in Nov. 1892. The village developed faster than Pedong and by 1895 there were 139 Catholics in the village while Pedong had only 20.

Soon groups of Lepchas and Nepalese from villages of Dokha, Kachim, Kiangtchen and Lengtse became Catholics. In 1895, the Government leased out another piece of land at Lengtse to the Catholics but refused permission to the protestants who wanted to establish a school there. Similarly the Catholic Mission was forbidden to establish centre in Kalimpong where they were offered land and house by converts; likewise at Nok where there were a few Catholic families. The authorities were imposing on the mission the limits where they could work.[17]

The leased land belonged to the Government while the people were only cultivators who paid about 4 annas per acre by way of rent. The mission was not allowed to sub-lease the land or claim any tithes. It had to maintain itself only on donations. The mission superior however could nominate the village chief of Maria Basti.

By 1900 the parish of Pedong had two sub-stations at Sakiong and Kachim totalling together 102 Catholics. The parish of Maria Basti with sub-centres of Lengtse and Kagay had 192 faithfuls.

Education, health care and social assistance could not be developed in a larger scale than the missionaries carried out, due to the stringent regulations that the Government imposed on them and also due to lack of resources. No subsidy or grants-in-aid were allotted to their schools as it was for the Scottish Mission establishments.

Nevertheless, by 1900 the schools of Sakiong and Kachim had 45 boys and the three schools of Maria Basti, Lengtse and Kagay totalled 60 boys. Pedong and Maria Basti maintained orphan boys while the orphan girls were looked after by individual Catholic families. The orphanages also served as boardings for boys of outlying villages. When the orphans were married, the mission met all the expenses of the marriage celebration and that of setting up of a new home.

At Pedong the missionaries set up a little hospital. Sick persons from outlying villages were treated there.

Most of the Catholics were either Lepchas or Nepalese. Of the two groups the Nepalese appeared to have impressed the missionaries more, with their piety and serious acceptance of their moral obligations.[18] The fact that for the Nepalese to become Christian meant breaking with the caste system and be considered an outcaste, implied that they had to make a courageous decision and took their new faith seriously. The missionaries hoped that one day they would be able to introduce Catholicism into Lhasa through these fervent Nepalese who could easily move in and out of Tibet.[19]

Conclusion

Till the twentieth century, the Roman Catholic missionaries were prevented from exercising their ministry in Darjeeling district due to several factors. Lack of personnel and resources did not permit the Capuchins to work among the local population while the Protestant Scottish Mission steadily increased its role in the educational development of the entire district, with the exception of the Terai. Jurisdictional disputes delayed by several decades the Catholic apostolate in the hill. Nevertheless, the institutions of Loreto, St. Joseph's College and St. Helen's, Kurseong, did a yeoman service in educating an elite group of pupils who would later become the leaders not only in Darjeeling but also in Nepal, Sikkim and Bhutan. Moreover, they established the first nucleus communities of Catholics who would later form the leadership for more flourishing churches of the twentieth century.

While the Scottish Mission exclusively enjoyed vast resources from the Government to be spent on education, the Catholics were prevented from establishing mission centres and schools in the outlying villages. The British government followed the policy of parcelling out the whole of the north-east India between various Christian denominations and the Roman Catholics were excluded from various territories until India got its independence.

Notes and References

1. Ever since the growth of Muslim power in the Middle East, the Christian powers of Europe were in search of Christian allies in Asia. Legend of "Prester John", a powerful Christian King was popular and one of the aims of the Portuguese explorers was to reach his court and make an alliance against the Muslims.

2. Records of the expeditions of the Franciscan Odoric of Friuli (1328-29), of the 17th century Jesuits D'Andrada, Gonzales de Souza, John de Olivayre, Francasco de Azevedo, John Grueber and others. have come down to us. (cf. A.Launary, *Histoire de Mission du Tibet*, I (Paris, 1904), pp. 19-31).
3. For a brief narrative cf. H. Josson, (1921) *La Mission du Bengal Occidental I* (Brugess), pp. 73-74.
4. A clear description of the Capuchin apostolate in Tibet and Nepal is given by : Fulgentius Vannini, (1976). *The Bell of Lhasa*, (N. Delhi).
5. M.M.Colmcille. *First the Blade; History of the IBVM. (Loreto) in India 1841-1962*, (Calcutta, 1968), pp. 54-72.
6. For the correspondence between Carew, Hartmann and Rome over Darjeeling, cf. Propaganda Archives, Scritture Referite nei Congressi - Indie Orientali, 10, pp. 1084-92; 1353-56.
7. Cf. E.C. Dozey, (1922) *A Concise History of the Darjeeling District*, (Calcutta), p. 108.
8. This school for Nepali girls could not compete with the institutions run by the Scottish mission which had practically a monopoly of the vernacular schools of the entire district since they alone enjoyed the grants-in-aid from the government. Only in 1920s did the Loreto nuns successfully run the St. Theresa's Nepali Girls' school. cf. Colmcille, *op. cit.*, p. 146. On the role of Scottish mission in the field of Education, see L.S.S.O' Mally, (1907) *Darjeeling* (Calcutta), pp. 171-77; J.A. Graham (1897). *On the Threshold of three closed lands*, (Edinburgh) 84-91; J.R.Minto, (1974) *Graham of Kalimpong*, (Edinburgh) 38 f.
9. Ignatius Persico, later made bishop as Vicar Apostolic of Agra died in Rome in 1896 as Cardinal.
10. George Kottuppallil (1983). *Origin of the Catholic Church in Bengal;* a Doctoral dissertation (Rome), pp. 223-46.
11. *Ibid.*
12. Josson, *op. cit.*, 89f.
13. Josson, *op. cit.*, 92.
14. *Ibid.*, 96.
15. For a detailed account of the efforts of the MEP missionaries to enter Tibet through Assam, Bhutan and Arunachal, see, A.Launay, *Histoire de la Mission du Thibet*, p.98f.
16. Born at Meuse (France) on 16 Oct. 1826 Auguste Desgodins became a priest in 1850 and joined the society of Foreign missonaries of Paris in (1854). See Launay, *Histoire*, 226 F.
17. Cf. Launay, *Histoire*, 266 f.
18. Launay, *Histoire*, 365.
19. *Ibid.*

CHAPTER 10

Pattern of Religion Among Arunachal Tribes with special reference to the Adis

J.N. Chowdhury*

The territory of Arunachal Pradesh, raised to the status of a Union Territory in January 1971, and to the statehood in February 1986 comprises an area of 83,578 square kilometres and a population of 6,28,050 (according to the 1981 census), lying along the southern slopes of the eastern extremity of the great Himalayan barrier. Out of the total area, the Himalaya constitutes about 70,000 square kilometres and the rest forms the foothills or the terai regions across the Brahmaputra. The territory rises in mighty convolutions of ridges and spurs, the crest line running along the extreme north, bound by eternal snow, and the bottom fringed by tropical rain forests about 50 kilometres broad. The whole area is highly jagged, presenting a formidable terrain, and regarded as one of the most difficult regions of the world. Arunachal is naturally marked into distinct divisions by its mountain ridges generally running north to south, and the river systems running through each region. Until recently, unsurpassable mountain walls stood between different ethnic groups inhabiting the terrain, condemning them to live in comparative isolation from each other through the corridor of historical time.

---

* Retired Librarian, Arunachal Research Department Library, Shillong.

People

There is said to be about 20 major ethnic groups, occupying what has been called by B.S.Guha[1] the North-Eastern zone of tribal settlements in India, the other two being the Central zone and the Southern zone. All are not equally important, nor in the same state of development in the scale of material progress. With regard to racial affiliation, they have been variously described as Indo-Mongoloid, Proto-Mongoloid, Paleo-Mongoloid and so on. They are said to belong to the so-called Tibeto-Burman group of languages with traces of Austric influence as confirmed by the *Imperial Gazetteer of India*. Referring to the tribes of North-Eastern zone, Guha observed : "In this group there is no tribe that is purely in the hunting or food gathering stage".[2]

Guha obviously chose to ignore the Sulungs spread over the Kameng and Subansiri regions, who until very recently, and still very largely, are in food-gathering stage, and in a state of semi-nomadism. The tribes are primarily agriculturists with the Apa Tanis of Subansiri being most noted for their highly efficient methods of cultivation with irrigation and terracing, though ploughing is unknown. The Khamptis of Lohit, comparatively recent migrants from the Bor-Khampti region, near sources of the Irrawady in Upper Burma, have known low-land farming, and follow it extensively in comparatively flat lands beyond the Kamlang river, their present home. The rest of the tribes preponderantly stick to the shifting method of cultivation, locally called *jhuming,* merely a variation of the *slash-and-burn* method known the world over, particularly among tribes. Among other distinguishing features noted by Guha among the tribes of the North-Eastern zone, 'Hereditary Priestly Shamanism' is widespread with Pile-dwelling and institutions of bachelors' dormitories, notably among the Adis of Siang and the Noctes and Wànchos of Tirap.

The Adis have known since time immemorial a highly centralised and democratic authority in the form of Councils of Elders, called *Kebang* in their dialect. The *Buliang* of the Apa Tanis of Subansiri wields less centralised authority, but is effective nevertheless with power of mediation in times of crisis. The Noctes and the Wanchos, as also the Khamptis and Singphos, and distinguished by hereditary chieftainship and highly stratified societies forming into distinct classes.

Religious and Cultural Profile

Verrier Elwin divided the Arunachal tribes culturally—the divisions hold true in respect of religion also -- into three main areas.[3] The first area comprising tribes such as Monpa and Sherdukpen in Kameng, the Memba and Khamba along the international border in upper Siang, and the Khampti and Singpho in the lowland areas of Lohit came under Buddhist infuence very early. The second cultural area broadly extends from eastern Kameng through Subansiri, Siang and Lohit and includes what is called the 'central block' of tribes comprising Bangni (actually the western branch of the Nishi) in eastern Kameng, the Nishi (formerly Dafla, a term which they now resent), Hill Miri, Sulung and Apa Tani in Subansiri, the various branches of the Adi stock (formerly Abor) in Siang, and finally the three distinct divisions of the Mishmi tribe in Lohit, namely Taraon (popularly known as Digaru), Kaman (popularly Miju) and Idu (popularly termed Chulikata). The third cultural and territorial group comprises the Nocte Wancho and Tangsa of Tirap. A small population of Lisu who came across the international border between Burma and India as recently as around 1941 is also found in Tirap.

These divisions cannot be looked upon as exclusive with ramifications extending on both sides of the border line, though 'a number of definite cultural traits' distinguish them. Early British explorers actually found little to discriminate between the tribes, and included all under a blanket term, Abor.

The Buddhist tribes under the first grouping noted above again fall into two distinct categories. The author of this paper, commenting on the presence of Buddhism in Arunachal, noted as follows in one of his publications:

> We have to reckon (here) with a very interesting fact of history. The Mahayana School of Buddhism, which came to be collectively known as the Northern Buddhism entered Tibet possibly from Kashmir in the 7th century, and again found its way back to India among the Monpas and Sherdukpens of the Kameng district of Arunachal Pradesh probably via Bhutan. On the other hand, the Hinayana School, later called the Southern Buddhism, which had originally migrated to Burma from Ceylon, was carried back to India by the Khamptis and the Singphos.[4]

Ethnically, the Monpas and Sherdukpens are linked to people across the border to Bhutan in the west, and across the northern frontier, namely Tibet. Linguistic evidence undoubtedly points to very significant migration from the direction of Bhutan. Conceivably, prior to the coming of Buddhism, the Monpas and Sherdukpens as also the Memba and Khamba, followed a Shamanistic faith entailing belief in various categories of spirits and necromancy. Their religion must have been very much akin to the *Bon* of the pre-Buddhist Tibet. According to a legend, Buddhism was introduced into the Monpa country by no less a saint than Padmasambhava himself, locally known as *Lanon Rimpoche*. Whatever truth may be traced to this legend, history records that the Tibetan king Khrisrong-Ide-btsan welcomed Padmasambhava on his arrival on the soil of Tibet at a place called *Gung-thang* on the north bank of the Brahmaputra -- not perhaps very far from the Indian frontier -- in the eighth century A.D. It is also historically confirmed that a Monpa, Lodre Gyatso who studied at Tashilhumpo, Sera and Gyume monasteries in Tibet, and later became famous as Mera Lama, received a mandate from the great fifth Dalai Lama of Tibet (Nangwang Lobsang Gyatso, 1617-1682) to build a monastery for the *Gelugpa* sect in his native Monpa land. The monastery in Tawang with a capacity to accommodate 500 lamas still commemorate the hallowed memory of Mera Lama. Another momentous event in the history of Buddhism among the Monpas was the appearance of the sixth Dalai Lama (Tsangyang Gyatso) who went to Tibet from the Monpa land.

The Khamptis who adhere to the *Hinayana* school of Buddhism, as already noted, came across Burma in the not too distant past and brought their religion with them. The Singphos, comparatively at a lower level of culture, also migrated from the direction of Burma in recent historical time. Known to the Burmese as Kakhyens (and actually a branch of the Kachin tribe) originally lived in the hilly region between Patkoi and Chindwin rivers. They also brought their religion, Buddhism of the *Hinayana* denomination, with strong belief in *Nats* (spirits) from Burma. Incidentally, before the advent of the British, the Khamptis were the only tribe in Arunachal, credited with a script, related to the Tai language. They show great reverence to the Buddhist canonical literature, the *Tripitakas* preserved in their monasteries.

The central block of tribes in the second category with whose religious beliefs we shall be especially concerned in this paper, conforms to Guha's description of 'hereditary-Shamanism'. British explorer-writers, on the other hand, coined the term 'animist-Shamanist' to describe their religion. We shall try to show that these fixed notions are either too narrow to be true or fail to measure the depth of their feelings and their conceptual perception of values, though their rituals undoubtedly are dominated by the ecology of their physical situation. In other words, they are linked to their subsistence economy, *i.e.* agriculture. The tribes, included in this category, have many cultural traits and beliefs including their pantheon of gods and spirits in common. The Hill Miris, Nishis and the Apa Tanis, to a casual visitor to their land, will present a near similar appearance. All the three tribes gather their hair in front, and tie them into a bun, called *podum*, protruding over their forehead, and a bodkin or brass skewer passed through it. While the Hill Miris generally make a bushy knot of the hair over the forehead, and wear a leather fillet, studded with copper knobs, passed round the head, the Nishis secure the *podum* with a strap of yellow cloth wound round it. The Apa Tanis wear their *podum* in a finely plaited knot with a brass skewer stuck horizontally through it. All the tribes put on similar wicker-work hats on their heads or a sporting angle, the Apa Tanis having as an additional appendage, a tail of spliced cane. The Nishi and the Hill Miri live in very long houses, built of bamboo and cane, recalling the long-houses of the Borneo people in another part of the world. The Apa Tanis have very spacious houses built similarly on stilts.

In fact, Furer Haimendorf was inclined to treat the Nishi and the Hill Miri as one people.[5] He argued that the traditional genealogy included the Hill Miri in Dol group, which also comprised many Nishi clans, and was actually regarded as one of the three divisions of the Nishi tribe, namely Dopum, Dodum and Dal. The Hill Miris, however, contend that their ancestor was a brother and not a descendant of At Nia, the forefather of the Dol and the Dodum clans. All the Nishi groups traced their descent from Abo Tani, the mythical first man, whose son was Atu Nyah. This legend, in its variations, is common among the Apa Tanis, Sulungs, Tagins and the Bangrus, besides Nishi and Hill Miri, as noted above. The Apa Tanis, for instance, claim that their ancestor Taniba was a brother of Abo Tani, the resemblance of names being obvious.

The Tagins of Upper Subansiri, squeezed in between the Adis to their east and Nishi to the west, share cultural traits and religious beliefs with both. In the Adi pantheon of gods and spirits, *Donyie-Polo* (Sun-

Moon God) has a dominant position. About the Tagins, Elwin wrote : 'Tagin religion is also, in its general pattern, of the Adi type. There is the pantheon of gods headed by *Daini-Pol*, the Sun-Moon, who had below him a number of *Wiyus* (spirits)'. The Apa Tani, Nishi, Hill Miri and Tagin do not, however, possess the strong political organisation called *Kebang* and bachelors' dormitories, both for boys and girls, which distinguish the Adi. The *Kebang* of the Adis, Elwin believed, before it acquired secular character, was dominated by the priests, and was originally a priestly institution. The Adis of Siang are also credited with having a very rich oral literature in the form of rhapsodies, called *abang*, and *nytom* songs. These are all about their mythical lores, their gods and spirits, the creation of the earth, the origin of agriculture, and various rituals connected with it. The first attempt to record the folk-lore of the Adis was by B.S.Guha.[6] The Adi Folk Literature Research Centre, founded by a profound scholar, Bibhabasu Das Shastri, and former Director of Research, Arunachal Government, has since published two books, *Pume Dada Hoi Dada and Oyo Hei Ya* (1974) and *Bene Benbo* (1983), under the authorship of Tumpak Ete.

There is no evidence among the tribes, in the central block, of ever having had indulged in head-hunting. But the Apa Tani and the Nishi were known to have prized and carried away as war trophies, the severed hands of vanquished foes, when tribal feuds were the order of the day. The Apa Tanis kept and displayed the severed hands of their victims in their *nago* shrine, and performed the *Ropi* ceremony. The Nishis would cut off the left palm and the *podum* of the victim of their raid, and carry them to their village. The palm was then fixed to a tree, called *nila senge*, and arrows were shot at it. The ceremonies and sacrifice, known as *Ropi Tamu*, connected with the occasion, are too elaborate to be detailed here.

The Mishmis of Lohit, who also belong to the central group of tribes, are a more archaic people. They might have migrated from the side of Burma in pre-historic time. They had the reputation of having been turbulent, more so the Idu (*Chulikata*) branch of the tribe, and are notable particularly for their colourful weaving in which they excel, and profusion of silver ornaments of their women folk. Their religion, which consists mainly of sacrifice and propitiation of numerous spirits, does not call for special attention. Elwin expressed his final opinion about the tribe in the following words : "They have few social virtues and are the most individualistic of NEFA (Arunachal) tribes".[7] Indeed, their history is a long tale of interminable intra-tribal and intra-clan feuds.

We now come to the third division of Arunachal tribes inhabiting the Tirap district coming round to the south-east and then south in relation to the entire territory of Arunachal, and lying along the northern watershed of Patkoi which abut against the Himalaya. Geographically and ethnically, the dominant tribes, the Nocte and the Wancho, are related to the Naga tribes to their south-west. It is not surprising, therefore, that they had a strong tradition of head-hunting. Williamson, who was an Assistant Political Officer at Sadiya, noted in 1908, that 'they (Nocte) certainly take a pretty steady toll of human lives'. O'Callaghan (1920-27) also confirmed that 'There was much traffic in slaves for the purpose of sacrifice among the Patkoi tribes'. Next to the Nocte, the Wancho had similar tradition of head-hunting, and both are distinguished by their *morung* institutions (Bachelors' Dormitories). Both believe in a host of spirits who are subordinate to a principal deity. In case of Nocte, it is *Jauban*, also called *Jongban* or *Tesang*. It has two aspects, good and evil, and they identify the two aspects as *Kat Jauban* and *Wang Jauban* respectively. The Wanchos believe in the benevolent sky-god, called *Rang*, and a malevolent god of earth named *Baurang*.

The Tangsas have the tradition of having migrated across the Patkoi in search of cultivable land, and still have kinsmen across the frontier in Burma. Their religious beliefs are of no special interest. They also identify spirits who are well-meaning and those who are ill-disposed to mankind.

Discussion

There have been attempts by anthropologists at conjecturing the origin of religion among the primitive people, and, by implications, extending their theories to more advanced and so-called civilized people. As opposed to Tylor, Frazer, for instance, sought the origin of religion in magic. John H.King thought that ideas of ghosts and spirits were too sophisticated for rude men and he, therefore, posited a 'mana' stage preceding ideas of ghosts and spirits. Marett, on the other hand, conjectured that primitive people had a feeling that there were inherent occult powers in certain persons and things and it was the presence or absence of this feeling which cut off the sacred from the profane, the wonderland from the work-a-day world, it being the function of taboo to separate one world from the other. A.E.Crawley had a more ingenious theory. He identified religion with the vital instinct, *i.e.* the will to live. According to him, religion makes sacred what promotes life, health and strength Origin of religion is thereby reduced to 'psycho-biological process'. Lowie was prepared to go along with Crawley insofar as religion was postulated as entirely feeling divorces from 'religious behaviour'. Now, the above are specimens of some of the theories, and more can be listed.

We have, by now, become acquainted with the terms 'animatism', 'animism', 'shamanism', or the combination of the two, 'animism-shamanism', and a host of other terms. These terms serve more or less as labels often to justify one's preconceived notion about what he thought of the religion of a particular people. Such theories, are, therefore, constricting, for they might not be of use in helping one to grasp the depth of feelings of a person or people about their religion or its role in shaping their individual and social behaviour. For instance, we may not ever find out why the Neanderthal man, variously estimated to have lived 50,000 to 100,000 or more years ago, buried their dead and used 'grave-goods', unless it is thought that they believed in some sort of an after-life. With reference to palaeolithic caverns in France and Spain, it was concluded : 'It seems much more reasonable to regard such caves as Niaux and Gargas as sacred spots where primeval mysteries were duly celebrated and which had to be approached with solemn and esoteric rites'.[8] In this context, one may as well ask : how old is the religion?

Before we pass on to the religious perceptions and beliefs of Arunachal tribes, we may profitably linger a bit to consider some other theoretical postulates on the beginning of religion, and possibly clear some facile conclusions drawn by anthropologists and social thinkers. It is possible for instance, to notice some universal ideas and their near global distribution irrespective of the stages of development of a particular human society. A society may again have the most complex and complicated social structure which cannot be explained on the basis of its material possession. Ralph Linton gives the example of *Pidjendadjara*, a section of Australian aboriginals, whose material possession consists only of a mortar and a pestle to grind corns, and bow and arrows, but have the most complicated kinship system. On the question of religious perceptions, it is possible to notice a universal pattern rooted possibly in the psychology and mode of religious thinking based on symbolic reasoning. It is nowhere more evident than in the process of myth-making. It was Andrew Lang who was first to conclude that the conception of a deity 'need not be evolved out of reflections on dreams and ghosts'. He contended that 'some of the very simplest societies had, as important figures in their religious pantheons, deities endowed with very considerable power, who dominated over other supernatural entities so that monolatory, if not monotheism, existed among some of the lowliest tribes'.[9] Schmidt supplied examples of high-god conception among such simplest and archaic tribes as Tasmanians, Bushmen, Andaman Islanders, Semang of the Malay Peninsula, Congo Pygmies and some others of 'comparable grades'.[10]

We may now notice the prevalence of the conception of high god or gods among Arunachal tribes who otherwise distinguish between two grades of spirits or deities according to their malevolent or benevolent intentions towards mankind. The idea of evil spirits, of course, stems from primitive man's perpetual sense of insecurity and apprehension of loss of subsistence. In this sense, environment or, for that matter, ecology does have a profound influence in shaping man's perception of his material stituation and his spiritual yearnings. We shall have more to say on this aspect when we consider the ritualistic practices of Arunachal tribes, particularly that of the Adis. Here we may only profitably quote Elwin :

> For centuries the real ruler of the
> tribal people here has been environment, it
> has shaped their bodies, directed their
> arts, forced babble on their tongues; it has
> been their governor, their policy maker.[11]

But environment alone cannot explain wholly their deeper perceptions or urges, and, to that extent, we have to dismiss such dismal and sweeping view as expressed by Dunbar, also with reference to Arunachal tribe, the Adis of Siang. To quote :

> His untutored mind sees a demon everywhere
> in the sun and the thunder, the earth and the water.
> It is a spirit of evil that takes life from all
> things that have breath...And the beginning and
> end of his religion, in sickness and in health
> in see time and in war, in the agonies of death
> and in the burial rites that follow, is to appease the
> malevolent spirits of an unseen world.[12]

To say the least, Dunbar was carried away by the hyperbolic flight of his imagination. That some of the Arunachal tribes, if not all, have conception of a creator god who has supremacy over other lesser spirits, refute Dunbar's conclusion so speciously made. The Akas, (Hrusso in their own language), for intance, who live close to the Sherdukpens in Kameng, are ethnically and culturally different from them, and successfully withstood Buddhist influence. They have conceptualised a few deities mostly identified with the major forces of nature, such as the sky, the mountain, the earth and the water. The qualifying address of 'father' or 'mother'.indicates the sex of the deity. *Metz Au* is Father Sky; *Phu Au* is Father Mountain; *No Ain* is Mother Earth and *Hu Ain* is Mother Water. But they also have the conception of a deity who stands above all. He is *Tcharo* 'who is the benign ruler of human as well as animal kingdom'. To him supplication is made for earthly well-being and blessings. The Khoas, calling themselves *Bugun* in their language, live in a state of subservience to the Akas and are distinguished from them mainly by their distinctive dialect. They have the conception of an all powerful and benevolent deity called *Chamram.. Chamram* has a partiality for everything white including the animal sacrificed to him. The Mijis (in their own language *Dammai*) also live in Kameng, surrounded by Nishis, Akas and Monpas. Their religion is predominated by spirits either inimical or friendly. But they conceptualised a powerful deity *Jang-lang-nui* approximating the conception of a high god, who lords over other lesser spirits. The Nishis (former Dafla) of Subansiri, already mentioned above, have the conception of a benevolent principle behind creation, identified with *Ane Duini*, the Sun-Mother. She is the supreme mother overflowing with kindness. Everything grows and survives at her will.

We may note here in passing that visualising sun as goddess, *i.e.* female, is a characteristic of all Arunachal tribes. But they share this idea with many other Mongoloid tribes. More on this point later. Among all the tribes, however, the Adis of Siang (former Abor) make almost a metaphysical approach to the conception of a supreme deity, the hypothetical first cause, the enigmatic *keyum*, sometimes called the Great Mother. In any discourse on the *abang*, (the traditional repository of creation myths *etc.*) the Miri invariably opens with the invocation :

Keyum ken-mang-e yayng-ko
kero kamang-e yayang-ko

Translated, it goes as follows :

Keyum is unknown and unknowable
Kero is invisible and unknowable
Karo here is another name or attribute of *Keyum*.

In the Adi pantheon, a distinct order of creation, from higher to the lower, tracing back to the hypothetical first cause, is enumerated in their *Mosup-Abang*. According to this order of creation, the first concrete being to materialise out of the womb of the first cause, the *keyum*, is a compound deity *Sedi-Melo* (earth-sky), though their separate individualities can also be deduced from many myths woven around them. They are sometimes conceived as sister and brother and, as there were no others in the dawn of creation, they together started the chain of creation. The idea of the beginning of creation in similar incestuous relation run through the mythologies of many religious systems. We are easily reminded of Adam and Eve, or *Yama* and *Yami*, in our own Hindu mythology. Gallong, a separate branch of the Adi people, attributes the beginning of creation to *Sichi*, their name for the mother earth. In Adi mythology, *Sedi* and *Melo* lay united in close embrace until they separated when *Doniye* and *Polo* (sun and moon) 'chased away darkness that enveloped the universe before'.[13] The Miri who leads the chorus in the *ponung* dance, extols the Mother goddess in the following *nytom* song :

Doni oji takam ngo-lu,
Dongor olo takam ngo-lu,
Sedi gordung-è ketu-lu,
Oil komjing-è rei-dung,
Olo dakpang-è sisa-dung'
(Doni's children all are we,
Dongor's children all are we,
on the back of sedi
We the children are spreading well;
We the children are growing together).

For a diversion, we may recall the creation myth of 'Shinto', the original religion of the Japanese people. 'The God who originally founded the country is the God who descended from Heaven and established their (Japan's) state in the period when Heaven and earth became separated...' It is also, perhaps appropriate to refer, in this context, to Vedic conception of *rodasi*, the two worlds. *'Dyava-Prithivi* (sky-earth) is conceived as *pitara, matara, janitri*, besides being addressed separately as 'father' and 'mother'. The conception of the *sky-father* is also found among the Greeks; *Zeus-Pater* is no other than the Vedic *Dayus-Pitar*. As I mentioned above, in the process of myth-making, similar ideas, and almost identical imagery, have a ring of universality whether in so-called high or low religion or whatever the difference in the degree of their sophistication.

In his book *The Worship of Nature*, forming his Gifford lectures, Frazer is credited with the sweeping statement that, among the Mongoloid hill tribes of Assam, the worship of heavenly bodies, including the sun and the moon, is either absent or very little developed. Elwin thereupon commented : "Had he known of the assiduous interest of the Abors (Adis), Mishmis, Daflas (Nishis) and the other tribes in the heavenly bodies, he would have modified the opening statement". Elwin also points out that, although comparatively little attention is paid to the sun and moon as deities in the Naga and Buddhist areas, there is a strong cult of the great luminaries right through the central mountains, in the Lohit, Siang and Subansiri, extending up to eastern Kameng. Indeed, at a later stage of development of their religious ideas, *Donyi-Polo* assumed supreme eminence in Adi theology. We have again Elwin's testimony : "But today, *Doini-Polo* is the nearest approximation to a supreme deity known to the northern Adis. He reigns unchallenged in the heavens; he is the 'eye of the world'".[14] As we have mentioned earlier, *Donyi-Polo* (sun-moon) is sometimes conceived as a compound deity, though at other times, they are distinguished as separate entities. I have also mentioned incidentally above, that the Adis thought of Sun (*Donyi*) as female, and Moon (*Polo*) as male. The Nishis have the same idea; so have the Buguns (Khoas), Boris, the Idu-Mishmis, Singphos, and the Padams.

Outside Arunachal, the Angami and Sema Nagas and the Khasis who are Austric in speech, also conceive of Sun as female. The same idea prevailed among early Scandinavians and West-German race. It is to be noted, in this context, that the Mongoloid people generally, who live under cold and temperate climates, associate sun with life-giving energy. Because of sun, living creatures and plant life thrive on earth. Sun is, therefore, the great Mother. We may again refer to Shinto religion in which the sun-goddess occupies a supreme position. On the contrary, the Semitic race who originated in desert areas, attached greater importance to the Moon than to the Sun (though the Moon is masculine). The Bedouins believed that life was regulated by the Moon which condensed the water vapours and distilled the beneficent dew on the pasture and made possible the growth of plants. In the oasis, they grazed their flocks under the light of Moon. Hitti concluded, whether justifiably or not, that Moon-worship implies a pastoral society whereas sun-worship represents a later agricultural stage.[15]

Another idea, which has a global dimension, to which the Adis subscribe but which does not seem to be immediately connected with their physical situation, is the emergence of earth from a primeval ocean. We will prefer to quote Elwin : "It is remarkable that people who have never seen the sea nor even, so far as we can tell, large sheets of water, should have devised the idea of a primeval ocean from which all things have emerged."[16]

There is another idea which also has a global dimension, about the beginning of creation from a cosmic egg. The Hill Miris, the Akas (Hrusso), and the Khamptis subscribe to this notion. The Akas tell the story that, at first, there were only two eggs. But they were not ordinary eggs, for they were soft and shone like gold. They did not stay in one place, but went round and round. At last they collided and the eggs broke and opened. From one came the earth, and and from the other, the sky, her husband. Here again, we are confronted with the idea of the sky-father. We are also reminded here of the *Vedic* lore of creation where it has been told that *Hiranyagarbha* laid an egg, one half of which became the sky and the other half the earth. The eminence of this idea among Arunachal tribes seems to disprove Suniti Kumar Chatterji's contention that creation out of a cosmic egg is a typical Austric idea,[17] though it is true that the idea of cosmic egg is most widespread among the Polynesian group of islands, the *Hawali,* the Society Island and the Tahitis. We cannot resist the temptation of quoting a relevant extract from Hastings' *Encyclopaedia of Religion and Ethics* on the imagery of the sky and the earth being the first borns of creation:

> No historical or proto-historical motive can be assigned as the cause and neither migration of races nor diffusion of myths and folklore affords the slightest justification of this fact. The universality of the sky-god and the uniformity of his essential characteristics are logical consequence of the constant uniformity of the primitive systems of cosmogony.

What has been said in the above quotation applies also to the notion of the cosmic egg. Though Chatterji would have us believe that Aryans originally borrowed the idea from the Austrics who preceded them on the soil of India, it was present among the Greeks. According to Greek Rhapsodist cosmogony, after Aether and Chaos came the egg and Lucas called it the egg of light. Finally there issued from the Egg the first Orphic God. As it has been explained in Hastings' *The World Egg* is an expression of the profound thought that the universe is an organism, gradually formed from an original germ, in compliance with the same law governing every living thing.[18]

Before we pass on to the consideration of the ritualistic aspect of Arunachal religion, particularly among the Adis, we have to refer to the recurrence of the idea among the tribes of 'a vast personage' who sacrificed himself so that parts of his body were transformed into parts of this earth. This idea again seems to have a universal pattern recalling the famous *Purusha-Sukta* in the *Rig Veda*. It is not the story told that is important, but the unconscious symbolism which underlies it. The Apa Tanis of Subansiri, for instance, tell the story that human beings originally clung to the body of the giantess Kujum Chantu who of her own accord died, so that they would not fall off and be killed. 'Every part of her body became a part of the world and her eyes turned into the Sun and the Moon'. The Minyong, a branch of the Adi, has a slightly different story : 'At first, all was water; the earth was below. Even rocks were soft as wet mud. *Kayum-sedi-Nane Wiyu* (some kind of a spirit) looked all over the water and tried to make earth but could not..... There was a *Wiyu, Sedi-Irping-Puing Idum-Botte* (some kind of divine personage), who had always lived on the face of the Water. When they (waters) dried up, he had nowhere to live and he died of his own will. His corpse turned into a mountain. From his bones came every kind of tree, from his hair the thousand grasses on the hills and they spread as forests over the earth'. From this story it is not a great leap to *Atharva Veda' s* description of the earth as the base of the highest Brahman, the air his belly, the sky his head, the Sun and Moon his eyes, fire his mouth and the wind his breathing. Elwin's observation, in this context, is relevant :

> A more remarkable idea found in some NEFA stories is that of creation by sacrifice of transformation of some great personage into the world, an idea which echoes the famous Purusha-Sukta in the *Rig Veda*... This was the beginning and the macrocosmic idea of the world as a vast personage is frequently repeated.[19]

Later, the same *Purusha* was identified with the creator *Prajapati* in the Hindu mythology.

Having dealt with the mythology and theology of Arunachal tribes, we may now turn to the ritualistic aspect of their religion which will be seen to be connected more intimately with their subsistence economy. It is, perhaps, natural that it should be so because, on the level of mundane existence, the constant dread of losing their subsistence, coupled with the vagaries of nature, complicated their feelings and their response to reality. It is not surprising, therefore, that the ritualistic aspect of their religion should be dominated by the idea of sacrifice linked to supplication. Most of their rituals and *rites*, excepting eschatological rites, are connected, in one way or another, with fertility of soil, increase of agricultural produce, and cattle wealth which, after agriculture, constituted their worldly possession.

The idea of sacrifice in its diverse manifestations is also a part of all world religions. We may only refer in passing to the *paustika* of the Vedic Aryans. Winternitz notes that *paustika* was offered "at the building of a house, benedictions for ploughing, for sowing, for the growth of corn, and exorcism against field-vermin, spells against the danger of fire, prayers for rain used in rain-magic, numerous benedictions for prosperity of the herds of cattle *etc*."[20] The above description of *paustika* in its totality will also serve for describing the purpose behind numerous sacrifices offered by the Arunachal tribes. Within the limitation of space, I have to confine myself to two tribes only, the Apa Tanis and the Adis who are engaged in intensive cultivation.

Two important ceremonies among the Apa Tanis are the *morom* and *mloko*. As noted by Furer Haimendorf, there is reason to believe that *morom* is actually a fertility rite having close link with agriculture. The present author had an opportunity to be present on one occasion, and watch the progress of the ceremony. It is performed in winter after the rice crop has been harvested, and is the signal for the beginning of fresh agricultural cycle. Furer Haimendorf writes that the villages of Bela, Hari and Hang give the lead to the performance of *morom* in the month of December-January. The *Haja-Duta* group of villages follow it up in the months of February and March. An important feature of the *morom* relates to procession of young people, boys and girls, going from village to village, led by the village priest who waves a fan and throws handsful of husked rice grains on either side of the rice fields. Young people are known to perform symbolic dances on the occasion, sporting huge bamboo phallus.

This shows the association of *morom* with agricultural and fertility rites. Two kinds of sacrifices are made on the occasion. The one called *Un-pedo* is expensive as it calls for sacrifice and slaughter of at least five or six mithuns. Mithuns (*bos frontalis*) is the most valued cattle among the tribes of Arunachal and is in great demand for the purpose of sacrifice and payment of bride-price. It is a cross between buffalo and cow. *Un-pedo* sacrifice can be afforded only by the rich households, while *padu-latu* is for persons of limited means. It involves sacrifice of two or three mithuns. These sacrifices can be compared with the feasts of merit among the Nagas, but no extra privileges attach to those who perform the sacrifices.

The other most important celebration which assumes the character of a national day among the Apa Tanis is the *mloko*. Its connection with agricultural cycle is unmistakable. *Mloko* is celebrated each year at the beginning of the agricultural cycle corresponding to the months of March and April. Its character of a spring festival is emphasised by the fact that priests conduct the ritual at the clan altar, called *nago*, inside a garden within the village. Invocations are offered to *Kilo*, *Kiru* and *Kirliyari*, the last connected with the earth. Domestic animals such as the mithun, pig and also dog are sacrificed. Animal husbandry is not well-developed among the Apa Tanis who have to depend on neighbouring tribes for sacrificial animals. An important feature of the celebration which can be seen as a cohesive social force compensating for the lack of central authority among the Apa Tanis, is its rotatory nature. It is confined to a single group of villages each year. The cycle is supposed to begin with *Hang* group of villages passing to other groups in turn until it comes round the full cycle. The performing villages are under obligation to entertain lavishly visitors from other villages of the entire Apa Tani valley.

The distinction between supplicatory and propitiatory sacrifices seems to be rather thin and one may easily acquire the character of the other in course of observance as I hope to show from ritual practices of the Adis of Siang. The first major rite of the agricultural cycle, among the Adis, is called *aran* or *pombi*. *Aran* marks the completion of clearing and initial preparation of Jhum fields. Offerings are made to *Gumin Soin* (domestic spirits). Besides house spirits, there is also an exalted *Gumin Soin* who is the guardian spirit of the whole village. The method of sacrifice either of a mithun or pig is by strangulation. In the case of the pig, it is laid on its back with the head between two stakes, and is suffocated with the pressing of a piece of wood against its throat. The invocations, chanted during its sacrifice, have unmistakably a note of supplication. An incantation goes like this : *Doying Ginjing-è Ane Ginjing-è no takamem run-ne nok-ke amin-lok ngo-lu Siki Nane melang Doyi Bote-ne imo-tontu-la no-lum ngo-lu takame siki pombi-em bi-bi-dung etc.'* (Protect us Oh ! Doying Ginjing. All will be looking up to you and to your name. We are calling upon the god of fields also, inviting him to the feast. To you we offer the *pombi aran* offerings.... Oh ! deity of the hearth and deity of fields take us unto your protecting care).

The spirit of supplication is even more clearly reflected in the following incantation recorded by Furer Haimendorf :

> *Doying-Bote, Kine-Dene Shidkin-kede*
> Sky God, earth spirit, earth deity
> *no-lu takamen shi-lo kombe invi-dung*
> for you all we always celebrate the *kombi* (also *pombi*)
> *no-lu takam, Doying-Angong, no-lu takam*
> for you all, sky god, for you all *dakum*
> *ngo-lum ai-ala apinam*
> give us kindly good crops.

Following the first phase of weeding of the field, the women of Adi village perform what is known as *lune solung*. A chicken is sacrificed near the granary and the blood is strewn around it. Furer Haimendorf also mentions a ceremony, called *etor*, connected with the fencing-in of fields. But constructing fences is not thought enough. Offerings to *Agam*, lord of the animals, must be made to ensure safety of the fields. 'On this occasion too, pigs and fowls are sacrificed'.

The climax to Adi rituals appears to be *luttor solung*. It is clearly intended for the prosperity of the cattle wealth. The ceremony takes place just before the final weeding, 'when the rice plants are about teh inches high'. Furer Haimendorf significantly remarks that, though set into a definite phase of the agricultural cycle, the rites illustrate the importance of the breeding of cattle (i.e.mithun). The households possessing mithuns (which generaly move about in a semi-wild state at other times) collect them from the jungles and bring them together into the yard and tie them to posts. Some magical importance is attached to the posts to which the animals are secured. A fine of one mithun is imposed on anyone wilfully damaging a post. This part of the ritual has a clear parallel to the increase ceremony performed by some Australian aboriginals such as the *Karadjeri* tribe. It is of interest to quote Hastings: "rudimentary conception of sacrifice set forth in *intichiuma* ceremony (increase ceremony) formed part of magico-religious cult at least as early as the Aurignacian culture period in Western Europe".[22] We are told that Vedic Aryans as cattle breeders used to perform it (*paustika*) for the prosperity of the herds of cattle *etc.*[23]

Before I conclude I should also, perhaps, make a passing reference to the *mopin* ceremony of the Gallong, a branch of the Adi tribe. *Mopin* is traditionally traced back to the mythical *Tani* (sort of first man on earth) who performed the ceremony, and obtained the blessings of *Mopin* who showered him with all kinds of seeds for cultivation. The celebration takes place in March-April signalling the beginning of the agricultural cycle. Sacrifice of mithuns is an inevitable part of the ceremony. But unlike the Padam-Minyong, (other major branch of the Adi tribe) who kill the animal by strangulation, the Gallongs dispatch it with an axe. A feature of the fanfare, connected with the celebration, is that everyone applies powdered rice-paste liberally to each other's face.

Notes and References

1. B.S.Guha, (1937). *An Outline Ethnology of India*.
2. *Ibid.*
3. Verrier Elwin, (1959). *A Philosophy of NEFA* (Calcutta :Oxford).
4. J.N. Chowdhury, (1971). *A Comparative Study of Adi Religion* (Shillong : Director of Information and Public Relations).
5. C.Von Furer-Haimendorf, (1947). *Ethnographic notes on the Tribes of the Subansiri Region* (Shillong; Govt. of Assam).
6. B.S. Guha, (1964) *Mosup-Abang* (Shillong : P.C. Dutta).
7. Elwin, *op.cit.*
8. James Hastings (Ed.),(1921). *Encyclopaedia of Religion and Ethics* Vols. 4,9,11,12.
9. Edward Norbeck, (1961). *Religion in Primitive Society* (Calcutta : Asiatic Society).
10. *Ibid.*

11. Elwin, *op.cit.*
12. G.D.S.Dunbar, (1938). *Other Men's lives : A Study of Primitive People.*
13. Sachin Roy, (1960). *Aspects of Padam-Minyong Culture* (Shillong : Sachin Roy).
14. Verrier Elwin, (1958). *Myths of the North-East Frontier of India* (Shillong : Anupam Dhar).
15. Philip K. Hitti, (1961). *The History of the Arabs* (London : Macmillan).
16. Elwin, 1958, *op.cit.*
17. S.K.Chatterji, (1948). *The Cultural Heritage of India*, Vol. I.
18. Hastings, *op.cit.*
19. Elwin. *op.cit.*
20. M.Winternitz, (1927). *A History of Indian Literature*, Ist edition, Vols.1 & 2 (Calcutta : Univ.Press).
21. Roy, *op.cit.*
22. Hastings, *op.cit.*
23. Winternitz, *op.cit.*

CHAPTER 11

Indigenous Faiths and Practices of the Minyongs

Tamo Mibang*

The Minyongs are one of the prominent sub-tribes of the Adis inhabiting East Siang and West Siang districts of Arunachal Pradesh. The Minyongs occupy a vast stretch of hills and forests covering an area of approximately 300 square kilometres bounded by snow-covered Takek Adi (Mountain) to the North, Yamne river to the east (Padam Land), Siyom river and Gallong land to the west and as far as Sika-Bamin, Oyan and Debing-Depi to the south.

The northernmost Minyong village is Pangkang and Debing-Depi are the southernmost. The principal villages are: Rigs, Pangkang, Dosing, Parong, Riu, Komsing, Rumgong, Jomo, Mopung, Molon, Yosing, Yogong, Kerang, Kaying, Paksing, Tumbin, Mori, Jomlo, Pangin, Kebang, Yemsing, Rottung, Renging, Mirem, Ladum, Rani, Ruksin, Rayang, Yagrung, Mikong, *etc.* More than 40 thousand persons live in this region preserving their indigenous faiths and cultures. The expression "Indigenous faith" has been defined in the Arunachal Pradesh Freedom of Religion Act 1978 (Act No.4, 1978) as follows :

> Indigenous faith means such religious
> beliefs and practices - including rites,

---

* Reader in History, Arunachal University, Pasighat, Arunachal Pradesh.

> rituals, festivals, observances, performances, abstinence, customs as have been found sanctioned, approved, performed by the indigenous communities of Arunachal Pradesh from the times these communities have been known and includes Buddhism as prevalent among the Monpas, the Kambas, the Khamtis and the Singphos, Vaishnavism as practised by the Noctes, the Akas and nature worships including worship of Donyi-Polo as prevalent among other indigenous communities of Arunachal Pradesh.

The Minyongs believe in the existence of a super-natural being, who is all powerful, omnipotent, and whose existence is even beyond the reach of modern science and technology. Everything that exists in the universe exists through Him. He is called *Donyi-Polo.* The Hindus call Him *Bhagavan* as the Muslims call Him *Allah* while the Christian call Him God. As a matter of fact, the physical-celestial body -- the sun and the moon -- are also called *Donyi-polo* by the Adis. In wider connotation *Donyi-polo* is the common spiritual authority of the Adis.

The supernatural world of the Minyongs consists of supernatural beings and spirits of dead persons. Some are male and others female such as *Kine-Nane, Ute-poro* (goddess of wealth and prosperity), Epon-ejang (god of wild animals), *Banji-Banmang* (god of hunting), *Adi-among uyu* (spirits of jungles), *Urom*(spirits of dead persons), and *Nipak-Porak* (common evil spirits). "in the sphere of religion", says Sachin Roy, "fundamental beliefs go back to the dawn of civilisation. All objects around them were to them as animate as themselves; they lived in a world where everything was living with invisible spirits presiding in them. Animatism, animism and supernaturalism came to basic ingredients of Adi-religion".[1] Sometimes, if offended, they act and behave like human beings by taking revenge on the offending human beings. For instance, *Asi-among uyu,* when offended, takes revenge against the offending person(s) causing serious illness; sells the soul of the person to other evil spirits from one jungle to another. It is called *Asi-among kinam* (or ailment of the jungle). They also cause *Ammo Kinam* (failure of the crops), cause damages to the houses by lightening and similar other calamities. Such abnormal behaviour of the supernatural beings is softened by performing appropriate rites and sacrifices with fowl, pig, cattle, mithun, *etc.*

The spirits of the dead form a separate category in their supernatural world. They are called *urom*. The Minyongs believe that every individual, after death, turns into a spirit and leads an ethereal existence, though the spirit occasionally shows itself to a particular person in the shape of the dead person. Sometimes, it causes illness to human beings, which is called *urom-kanam*. Generally, such illness lasts for 2 to 3 hours and in certain cases up to 2 to 3 weeks. They are called *Nipong-urom* (female spirits) and *Taleng urom* (spirits of the sky). A spirit remembers its friends, kinsmen, even belongings and occasionally appears before them in dreams.

Though an ordinary person cannot see a spirit either in daylight or at night, there are some people in the society who possess certain spiritual qualities and are well conversant with the languages of the spirits as well as with all technicalities of religious rites of the society. They are called Miris. Apart from medicines, an ailing person is cured through a ceremonial performance called *ipaknam*, or offer of prayer to demons and spirits of which the Miris are the custodians. On such occasions, they go on chanting hymns throughout the night tracing out the spirits responsible for causing sickness to the person. They passionately appeal to all sects of spirits to heartily accept their offer and to return the soul to the house. All the family members and other relatives spend the night with them. It is called *Miri boliknam*. One who falls asleep, dreams of returning a dog, fowl, or a pig to the house. Then it is presumed that the soul of the ailing person has come back to the house.

The next morning, in accordance with the advice of the Miris a *puja* is offered; the altar being made of variety of wild leaves. A mithun or pig with some fowls are sacrificed near the altar. The Miris and the Mijik use the entrails of fowl' livers as signs of their forecast. After completion of these formalities the Miris restrict the diets of the ailing person who is asked to abstain form taking liquor, pork, wild boar meat, chillies, variety of vegetables and even salt for a specific period, and also to refrain from going near the rivers and jungles. It is called *nyionam* or observance. But there is no separate Miri class in the society. Anyone may become a Miri at any period if he/she is liked by the spirits. The Minyong society has been witnessing this phenomenon since time immemorial.

The Mijik is one who locates the evil spirits by studying the liver of a chicken. He also occasionally meets the spirits in dream. So he asks the family members to perform *ipaknam* or offering of sacrifice to certain deities responsible for the sickness. In most cases he initiates the *ipaknam*. A pig and some fowls are sacrificed to propitiate the spirits. Such performances are not only psychologically beneficial but also cure the ailing and other physically disabled. Sometimes, even a fractured leg or head is completely plastered and cured by an Adi Miri which is a direct challenge to a modern orthopaedic specialist.

The Minyongs believe that every material object has a soul. If anybody commits an offence by stealing someone's fowl or mithun he is to give an additional poultry or mithun for sacrifice. If anybody steals a string of beads, he must in addition to the compensation for theft, give a pig or fowl, to persuade the soul to return into the necklace.

In case of land disputes between two parties, a ritualistic oath (*peki-Nikki Sinam*) is administered to the parties involved. Soil is accepted as the medium of justice. A handful of soil is taken out by both the parties from the disputed area and is thrown at each other and then eaten up by the two parties in the presence of the village members. After a short period of time the guilty one is believed to vomit blood and his urine, stool *etc.* also become blood before he dies, whereas the righteous person enjoys longevity of life.

They also perform a ritual called *Rogum sinam* against bad omens. This is performed when one of the family members narrowly escapes an unforeseen accident like attack by wild animals or snakes from trees or have bad dreams. An altar is made with a variety of wild leaves and bamboos. A fowl or pig is sacrificed at the altar in order to drive away the evil spirits and to bring back the soul of the members to the house. Guests are not allowed to enter the house and the family observes *genna* for at least three days.

The Minyongs celebrate a number of festivals such as *Unying*, *Mopun* and *Solung*, which are considered vital to the well-being of the individual, the family and the community. The sacrifice of mithun, pig and fowls is common during festivals; rice beer is abundant in every family and a number of guests are entertained by every family. Every member sings, dances and enjoys *pooung*. *Unying* is celebrated during January-February to mark and greet the new year; *Mopin* during April to offer prayer to the goddess *Kine Nane* for healthy crops and then

Solung during September to offer prayer to *Kine Nene* for rich harvesting and prosperous life. Every mother advises her children to enjoy the festivals joyously and she herself performs her ritual offering of meat, egg, and *Apong, etc.* to *Agung-Agam Uyu* (goddess of wealth and prosperity). It is the strong belief of the Minyongs that during festival many known and unknown guests including gods, goddesses and even evil spirits visit their homes who are supposed to be appeased.

During the *Unying* festival, some issueless couples perform a ceremonial dance called *Roja-Ganam.* The objective is to get the blessing for a child from the Almighty God. An altar is erected in front of the house around which the close relatives perform a religious dance with swords and caps. The host-wife in male attire leads the dance. After the dance, a community feast is served to the people. The Adi Minyong people believe that *Roja-Ganam* blesses the couple with sons and daughters. In many cases it is believed to come true.

The Minyong *Kumsung* (granary) does always have various kinds of cereals. They believe that there is an unseen One, who looks after it and because of His existence only cereals have come into it. He is called *Kumsung Uyu* (god, the custodian of the granaries). An offer is made to Him annually in the form of fowl, dryfish, *apong, etting* (bread), *etc.* Sometimes a pig is also sacrificed. When such an offer is not made, He is believed to cause illness to the family members. To propitiate Him, a red cock is offered by the Mijik and the sickness is reportedly relieved.

Although they hardly worship any idol or image, they offer their share of worship to every object of nature -- to rain, sun, snake, wild animals and trees. During draught when crops fail and springs dry up causing scarcity of drinking water, they offer prayer to the Rain god, called *Pedong Panam.* A village Miri is engaged to perform the rites. He chants the traditional hymns; makes appeal to the Rain god in the *Dere* (boys' dormitory) in front of the gathering crowds and goes on chanting;

> *Melo ke tene getung ke,*
> *Taka tene getung ko;*
> *pirbo e kaju kaju; alangku.*
>
> (It is my traditional and lovely cap, with it I appeal to you; Oh, Rain God, come, come and follow him in chorus: shower the earth with water.) The villagers follow him in chours:

> *Dotk a Tikra ra ra,*
> *Done dobude boot boot;*
> *Tiklinge domire teri likla yika,*
> *Tikdonge yari a pelop likla yika.*
> (Oh, frogs, support us, you also sing; bring
> down torrential rain to the earth; let storm
> come; let lightning create rain; we are longing for rain.)

They perform *Donyi-Bonam* (offer of prayer to the Sun God) also during the rainy season, when crops are destroyed and communications disrupted due to flood. The Miri goes on chanting:

> Doney e dadam delori delong;
> Bomonge kaju kaju alongkuka.
> (Oh, Almighty Sun; come, come soon; we all
> heartily invite you)

The Miri wears a special white cap, (*Metpung-Dun'lup*) made of bamboo; holds bow and arrow to kill the crabs, frogs, *etc.* responsible for continuous rain. He sings *miri* whole night and appeals to the Sun God for light and heat. He then forecasts the day and time when light would appear and days will be sunny. The effect of the *Donyi-Bonam* is often witnessed by them.

Whatever the nomenclatures the Minyongs have their own religion. They have a rich culture and tradition. Their religion is an important part of their identity. As a matter of fact, under the patronage of some influential local members, a *Donyi-Polo* Mission (a social organisation) is being set up at Itanagar, the capital of Arunachal Pradesh, in order to revive the traditional faiths and practices and to popularise the cult of *Donyi-Polo* among the simple Arunachal tribals and to protect them from conversion and thereby to evolve a recognised religion of their own. At the congress of the International Association for Religious Freedom (I.A.R.F.) held at New Delhi in February 1985 the Mission authority urged upon the world body to recognise *Donyi-Poloism* as one of the religions in the world.

Notes and References

1. Sachin Roy, (1960). *Aspect of Padam-Minyong Culture*, (Shillong : NEFA), pp. 235-36.

CHAPTER 12

The Doyas : A small Community of Bhutan

Bimalendu Majumdar*

Introduction

This paper is an attempt to describe some aspects of the religious and social practices of the Doyas of Tapakhan, a village in western Bhutan. It is mainly based on information obtained during the field investigation in November 1979 and through several interviews during 1973-81 at Totopara, an Indian village bordering Bhutan. Secondary sources like published books and survey reports have also been used.

The author became curious about the Doyas while he met some of them at Totopara and got some interesting information about them from the Totos, in 1975. Since then he made several attempts to go to Tapakhan for an on-the-spot field investigation there, but nobody from Totopara agreed to accompany him on the plea that the Doyas do not allow any stranger to enter their village. After repeated efforts, late Dinesh Toto -- the *Gapu* (headman) of the Totos[1] and his wife kindly agreed to accompany the author. The author went to Tapakhan with a team led by late Dinesh Toto (Who was also visiting the Doya village for the first time in his life), one Nepali 'witch doctor', who had already paid some visits to the Doya village and Dinesh Toto's family.

---

* Freelance researcher, Silpasamitipara, Jalpaiguri.

The Doyas are a little known people till today. It was D.Sunder who for the first time mentioned the name of Doyagaon in connection with the trade relations of the Totos, in his survey and settlement report.[2] C.C.Sanyal wrote a few lines about them in his book *The Meches and the Totos of North Bengal*[3]. B.K.Roy Burman, at the time of his field study at Totopara, had also recorded some information on the Doya tribe.[4] So did B.Chakraborty in his book on Bhutan.[5] Michael Aris, also gives some information about the village of the Doyas in one of his books.[6] He classified the Doyas as the 'gDang' group of people of Western Bhutan. One short article was published on the Doyas of Dorokhan, Dunkheng in the *Kuensel*, the official newspaper of the Government of Bhutan in 1987.

Background Information

The Doyas were the next-door neighbours of the Totos, inside the territory of Bhutan, till the early decades of this century. During the present investigation none of the Doyas could provide any information about the origin of the name of the tribe. They called themselves *Doiya*. A section of the tribe introduced themselves as *Roiya* (which may be a variation of pronunciation). The Totos called him *Doiya-bei* or *Daiya*, which means slave (of Bhutan). In this connection it may be mentioned here that the Doyas have an intimate relationship with the Totos, as a frontier tribe. They also used to maintain social and ritual relations among themselves. It appears from the previous records and information provided by the respondents that both the Totos and the Doyas were the *Zapo* (slave/serf) of the Bhutanese Government in the past. They required to render free labour in need of the Government as a part of their duty. The only difference was that the Totos were engaged in the duty of *Hura* (forced porterage for carrying the essential commodities of the Bhutan Government from the markets of Duars), while the Doyas were engaged to carry the forest produces within the territory of the Bhutanese hill areas.[7] A similar system of rendering service to the Government was prevalent in other states of the eastern Himalayas. Among the Reangs of Tripura a section of people were callled *Daiya Hazra* or attendant of the Roy, the Reang king,[8] which had great similarity with the position and role of the Doyas of Bhutan. However, the slavery system has been abolished from Bhutan, with the implementation of reform acts imposed by Jigme Dorji Wangchuk, the king of Bhutan, who ruled the country from 1926 to 1972. Since then the Doyas are enjoying a normal life like the other people of that country.

The Doya Village

The whole community of the Doyas is distributed in four separate villages, *viz.* (i) Tapakhan, (ii) Lam' Tekhan, (iii) Lutu-Kuch'chu, and (iv) Dorkhasiddim.[9] These are located in the inaccessible areas of western Bhutan.

Tapakhan, popularly known as Doyagaon is situated 15 kilometres away from Totopara on a shelf like valley of Tading of Samchi sub-district of Bhutan. The altitude of the village is about 2500 feet to 3500 feet above the mean sea level. It is situated at the confluence of river Amachhu (Torsha) and Luri, a turbulent stream from the west.

The Doyas and their livelihood

The village Tapakhan, solely inhabited by the Doyas, comprises only 65 families, with a population of about 280 persons of a completely mono-ethnic nature. The total population of Doyas is a little under 1000 with the number of men and women being almost equal. They belong to the Mongoloid race. They are of medium height, strong build, brown skinned and resemble the Bhutias in physical features. The houses of the Doyas are similar to those of the tribes of the north-eastern hill states. Due to their quarrelsome nature the settlement pattern is scattered.[10] The same cause of settlement pattern was found among the 'Abors' of Arunachal Pradesh by Verrier Elwin.[11] The Doyas have few utensils. They use one or two cheap metal pots for boiling their food, which is the main mode of their cooking. Bamboo pots are widely used for drinking and carrying water and liquor.

Orange is the main cash crop of the Doyas. They own as well as work in the plantations. They also grow betel leaves. They use their lands, located on the steep and precipitous slopes of the hills for rudimentary agriculture. Forest gathering, fishing and trapping are some subsidiary sources of their livelihood. Weaving is a decaying cottage industry among them [12] because the mill-made cloths are easily available at Totopara market. Their garments are similar to those of the traditional garments of the Totos. They have traditional trade relations with the Totos, which are gradually being shifted to the non-Totos. They are very much addicted to home brewed liquor and always chew betel leaves and nuts.

Religious Life

Religion has a very important role to play in the society of the Doyas and their priest, called *Gangupama* (*Gangu* = Priest, *Pama* = Man) plays a more vital role in their society than their headman. He is the religious head of the Doya society and performs all the religious functions right from the birth ceremony to death rites, in addition to his normal duties of worshipping the deities on several occasions.

The post of the priest is not hereditary but selective. The headman selects an efficient person as a new priest with the help of other senior priests and village elders. The priest does not enjoy any special facility other than a common villager.

Unlike the old days when the priest was the most powerful person of the Doya society, the head of their religious organisation and judge of the village, (just like the previous Toto head priest who is also called Subba or Kaji by the Totos) the Doya priest is losing his power to the Doya headman or *mandal* in modern times. The reason of this is the appointment of the Doya headman, as the *mandal* (secular chief of the village) by the government with the responsibility of administration, revenue collection, land distribution, *etc.* This has happened in the case of the Toto head priest-cum-judge as well.[13]

The deities

The chief deity of the Doyas is *Dzibdak-Doreng-Gong*, in short, *Dzibdak*, who is worshipped at the beginning of all religious functions. There are some minor deities as well -- like the god of jungle and the god of streams and rivers. They believe that if the deities are pleased, the Doyas will get good forest collection without any harm and the river god will save their homesteads, lands and orange plantations from the swallowing landslides. Like the Totos and the Bhutias, they also worship the source of water called Omchhu or Wangchhu, the belief being that if they do not do so, the source of water will dry up and they will not get water for drinking purpose or for irrigation. The Doyas do not make any image or statue of their deities, nor do they have any particular place for worship. They worship in the jungle as well as in their houses. They are 'animists'.

It is reported that, previously the Doyas used to perform their annual religious festival and worship along with the Totos on the top of 'Badoo' hills (*Itspal*) situated on the border of Totopara within Bhutan. It was abandoned by both the communities after a confrontation between them on the day of their annual worship.[14] Since then both the communities have begun worshipping their deities at their respective villages, according to a revelation in the dream by their superior deities.[15]

Gaiyu and the Hachat : The biggest festivals

It is found that the nature, season and duration of the biggest annual festivals of both the Doyas and the Totos are almost the same. The Doyas observe two annual religious functions, namely *Gaiyu* and *Hachat*. *Gaiyu* is observed in the second week of August. They observe it in their homestead or inside the houses. For this they offer sweet tubers (yams) and liquor to the god. Like the Totos they call this festival the small festival. It is comparatively less expensive than the *Hachat*.

The *Hachat* is the biggest festival of the Doyas which starts in the second week of September.[16] On this occasion, they put on new clothes and ornaments made of beads and coins. In this festival, the Doyas worship their goddess *Dzibdak-Doreng-Gong*[17] to whom they offer pigs, hens, sweet yams, and fruits of various kinds. The *Gangupama* sprinkles blood of the sacrificed animals, some home made liquor and a portion of offerings in the name of *Dzibdak* to all directions and chants incantations. A share is given to *Gangupama* as his honorarium, but no cash is given. The family members, their kins and family friends get together and take food and drinks. Food and drinks are also exchanged between close kins. The whole village becomes agog with community songs and dances.

This festival has a great similarity with the *Pak-Patang* or the first fruit plucking festivals of the Zemi Nagas of Arunachal and the festival of the Maiyu Totos of North Bengal as also with the Mango offering ceremony in Bengal.[18]

Since orange is the main cash crop and the whole economy of the Doyas depends on good prospect of the oranges they start plucking orange in the month of September by offering the first fruit to their chief deity, *Dzibdak*. Their nearest neighbourers, Totos, also perform their orange offering festival almost in a similar way.

There is no caste system among the Doyas, there being no difference between the priest and the common man. However, a kind of class system is emerging with the introduction of cash.

Recently efforts were made to preach Buddhism, the official religion of Bhutan among the Doyas. The Dungkhang office sent two Doya boys to Simtokha School and three more as *gelongs* (monks) to the *Samchi Dratshang* for this purpose.[19]

Some socio-religious activities

The socio-religious activities like birth, marriage and death are vital and unavoidable parts of any society, particularly among the preliterate communities like the Doyas. They observe these rites and rituals according to their traditional beliefs and social customs. These are as follow:

(a) *Childbirth* : There is no separate room among the Doyas for childbirth. Generally the sleeping room is used for this purpose. An experienced elderly woman assists the mother, during the delivery of a child. If any abnormality is found at the time of delivery, a village exorcist is called in. After performing the exorcism he prescribes the way out for the mother, which may not prove fruitful. Yet they have great reliance upon the exorcists. There is no ritual function in the childbirth. The child is given a name on the third or the seventh day according to the choice of the parents. On the naming day of the child, the *Gangupama* is called in for offering worship for the future prosperity of the child. The ceremony requires home-made liquor and a certain kind of sweet yam. A chicken may also be killed and its nails, beak and some meat along with some blood are offered to the evil gods, to appease them.

(b) *Marriage* : In fact there is no special ceremony for a Doya marriage. The elderly persons generally decide the matter. Then the girl is brought to the house of the boy. But before that, the bridegroom has to serve the family of the bride for about three years --- a system, which is now getting abolished. After completion of the said period, the groom is allowed to take the bride to his house. A feast is given among the kins of the boy and the girl and their family friends. Drink and meat are the main items of the feast. At least a cow must be killed for this purpose. The function continues throughout the day and night, followed by community songs and dances.

Praying for the peaceful life of the couple, the *Gangupama* performs a worship and chants *mundhums* (*mantras*) to the god *Dzibdak* and asks him for his blessings. The Doyas can marry any girl other than his own sister. Cross-cousin marriage is a general custom. Age is not considered at the time of their marriage. Any old man or woman can marry a younger one. Divorce and remarriage are allowed. Polygamy is found among them. The Doya headman (Kanja Doya) has six wives. The dignity of a Doya marriage is determined by the number of cows slaughtered for the feast and the number of invitees attending. This is similar to that of the Totos of West Bengal.[20]

The patriarchal system is now current among them. Marriage within their own community is customary. On the way to the Doya village, the author found one Doya mother and her daughter, married to two Nepali (*Kami*) brothers in their neighbouring village. Later, the author was informed that the women had been driven out of their village for some reason which was not known to the informant.

Marriage has no ritualisitc importance among the Doyas. The main aspect of Doya marriage is the gratification of the sexual urges and bearing of the offspring. But there is another aspect of the marriage, by which he or she strengthens the family by adding an additional labourer.

(c) *Death rites* : The Doyas have some peculiar rites after death. They keep the deceased for two days in the house. Thereafter, like the Lepchas,[21] the body is taken out by breaking the floor of the house, instead of through the door. Some of their kinsmen go to collect *Lek Tsing* (*Kimbu*) timber from the forest, for planking. These plankings are left in grave. They have no particular graveyard. They dig the grave adjacent to their dwelling house, so that the black fly can visit both the decomposed body and the living being, through the holes in between the stones, placed upon the grave. They believe that this will help to maintain communication with the dead man's spirit and appease it so that it causes no harm to his/her living relations. A hen or a cock (also a pig sometimes) is to be offered at the graveyard, according to the sex of the deceased.

If the deceased is a minor (*i.e.* less than seven years), then the unclean period will be observed for three days, but in case of an adult member (father, mother, wife or husband) this period will be observed for three years. After the end of this period, the *Gangupama* cleans the kinsmen by chanting incantations. There are also some other taboos for this period. For instance, one cannot go to others' houses and take any food and drink from anybody, except his family members. On the other hand, no member of another family touches any food and drinks offered by such unclean persons.

(d) *Tse-Akk* : On the eighteenth day of the expiration of the deceased, the final ritual called *Tse-Akk* is observed. On this day the relatives of the deceased and the villagers assemble and take food and drink. At least one cow and several pigs and hens are killed for meat. Some food, drink and water are offered as the last meal at the grave before the feast begins. The total carcass of a pig is offered too. They believe that this pig will lead the soul to the 'world of dead'. Earlier a man of the Toto community used to be invited to take away the carcass of the pig.[22]

After offering the last meal the *Gangupama* makes the last communication with the dead. With this function the *Tse-Akk* ceremony ends and the relatives of the dead are allowed to lead their normal life, except some restrictions which have to be followed in case of social life, till the expiry of three years.

Social organisation and social control

Like in other societies family is the smallest social unit of the Doya social organisation. The Doya families can be classified roughly into two types : simple and extended. The family of the Doya headman, Kanja Doya, is the largest extended family in the whole Doya village with his six wives and other unmarried family members including his would be son-in-law, who is the son of his younger brother.

(a) *Mandal or the headman* : The headman is the chief of the Doya village. The post is not hereditary. The *mandal* solves all disputes arising in the village. He contacts the government officials and neighbouring village headmen in need and for the betterment of the village. He also maintains inter-village relations to run their affairs undisturbed. All the land of the village is under his disposal. He distributes the lands and also disposes of the disputes over lands. At present they have been exempted by the Government of Bhutan from paying land revenues. But they are still bound to offer free labour to the headman. So, till now, the headman is the supreme authority, the centre of power of the Doya village. Of course, he performs the duties with the help of the village elders.

Like in the Indian villages, a statutory panchayat system has been introduced in the Doya village but the impact of this new system is negligible. People of the village are still dependent on their traditional village *mandal*. On the other hand, they show a great respect for the government officials and fear them too.

The Government of Bhutan has started some developmental projects like animal husbandry, agriculture, extension of animal transport services, surface communication *etc.*[23] It has also established a primary school (in English medium) and departmental extension centres at Bukka and Tading Bhutan, near Indian border. These are respectively about 10 and 15 kilometres away from their village. The Doyas rarely visit those centres due to their ignorance, lack of motivation towards the modernisation and the physical distance of the extension centres.

Notes and References

1. His original name was Gagepa. He informed the author that he had never visited Doyagaon till then. This in spite of their connections with the Doyas, there was no friendly relation with them, since an incident of war in the past at Doyamara (a place near Totopara).
2. D. Sunder, (1895). *Survey and Settlement of Western Duars*, Govt. of Bengal. He wrote in his survey report - "The Bhutias have a village at *Doyagaon* in Bhutan, about 8 miles North of Totopara, where they grow orange. The Totos bring oranges from there into the British territory..." Para-460.
3. C.C. Sanyal, (1972). *The Meches and the Totos of North Bengal*, (North Bengal University) p. 31.
4. B.K. Roy Burman, (1957). "Brief statement on the socio-economic situation in Totopara and perspective and programme of activities in Totopara welfare Centre" (Unpublished paper).
5. B. Chakraborty, *Bhutan*.
6. Michael Aris, 1st Ed. (1980). *Bhutan, The Early History of the Himalayan Kingdom* (Shahidabad: Vikas), pp. xvii-xviii.
7. "The Doyas : a unique ethnic group". *Kuensel* - July 25, 1987, Vol. 2, No. 29, p. 5.
8. B.K. Roy Burman, (1959). *Dynamics of Persistence and Change of a Small Community : The Toto*. Unpublished dissertation, Calcutta University, pp. 67-100.
9. Based on information provided by Kanja Doya, the present headman of the Doyas of Tapakhan (Doyagaon).
10. This is informed by Jeete Doya, a villager of Doyagaon, and the Nepali Shaman, who accompanied the author on his way to the Doya village.

11. Verrier Elwin, (1957). *India's North-East Frontier in the Nineteenth Century*, (Oxford) p. 155.
12. Michael Aris, *Ibid.*, pp. xvii-xviii.
    The dress which has been narrated by Michael Aris (garment of 'Toktop' male) is very much similar to that of the Doyas of Doyagaon (Tapakhan) and the Totos of West Bengal. The thread for manufacturing the clothes (made of the fibre of Nettle plants), had been widely used by the Doyas and the Totos in the past, but presently both the communities have given up the practice of weaving the cloths from the fibre of Nettles. This plant is still found in Totopara and Tapakhan areas.
13. Tsee' Rong Kaji (Toto) - The head priest of the Totos. He is the religious head of the Toto society and still now the *Kaji* (Judge) of the Toto social-organisation. In this regard, B.K. Roy Burman wrote in one of his papers : "Previously the offices of Kaji and Mondal were reported *to be* held by the same person. Three generations ago, after the territory was transferred to the jurisdiction of British from that of Bhurita, the office of Mondal was separated to cope with the growing complications of work" (*op. cit.*, p. 22).
14. This has been informed by late Dinesh Toto, the headman of the Totos.
15. There is a legend about confrontation between the Doyas and the Totos on the day of their annual worship, in the long past.
16. The Doyas have their own calendar like that of the Totos.
17. According to Kanja Doya, the Doya headman and one of their priests, the god *Dzibdak-Doreng-Gong* is at the same time a male and female god like the god *Itspal* or *Tsainjani* of the Totos and the *Purush-Prakti or Ardha-Nariswar* concept of the Hindu mythology.
18. The Hindu Bengalis worship before they eat mango and offer the fruit to their deity as mango is one of the delicious fruits and also the cash crop of a greater part of the undivided Bengal. There is also a practice of offering green mango with ground and fried rice on the last day of the Bengali year, in some parts of Bengal. This is called *Bhai-Chhatu*.
19. *Kuensel* - *Ibid.*, p. 5, para 22.
20. B.K. Roy Burman, *op. cit.*, p. 18. About the Toto marriage he wrote: "There are two forms of marriage - the more respectable one is *Baro-behao* (*Wama-denkhuri*) in which the whole village is to be fed with sacrifice of 5/6 cows. The other is *Chote-behao* (*Japaoa*) in which two cows or two pigs are sacrificed".
21. A. Moitra, (1974). *Sikkimer adibashi Lepcha* (Calcutta; A. Mukherjee & Co.), pp. 45-47.
22. This may be treated as the *Agradani* system of *Preta-sraddha* of the Hindus. The man who used to go to the Doya village from the Toto community to bring the carcass of the offered pig was treated as a very brave man by both the Totos and the Doyas, as he was sharing the carcass with the dead spirit.
23. *Kuensel* - *op. cit.*, p. 5.

Index

V

W

Y

Z